CRAFT OF CASE-MAKING AND CABINET-MAKING

The Modern Carpenter Joiner
and Cabinet-Maker

CRAFT OF CASE-MAKING AND CABINET-MAKING

G. Lister Sutcliffe, Editor

Associate of the Royal Institute of British Architects,
member of the Sanitary Institute, editor and joint-author of
Modern House Construction, author of *Concrete:
Its Nature and Uses*

Roy Underhill, Consultant

Television host of "The Woodwright's Shop",
author of *The Woodwright's Shop*, *The Woodwright's
Companion*, and *The Woodwright's Workbook*, and
Master Housewright at Colonial Williamsburg

A Publication of
THE NATIONAL HISTORICAL SOCIETY

The Modern Carpenter Joiner and Cabinet-Maker presented
up-to-date techniques and tools for its time. However, much has
changed since 1902. Not all materials and methods described in these
pages are suitable for the construction materials and tools of today.
Before undertaking any of the building, remodeling or other practices
described in these pages, the reader should consult with a reputable
professional contractor or builder, especially in cases where
structural materials may come under stress and where structural
failure could result in personal injury or property damage. The
National Historical Society, Cowles Magazines, Inc., and Cowles Media
Company accept no liability or responsibility for any injury or loss
that might result from the use of methods or materials as described
herein, or from the reader's failure to obtain expert professional
advice.

Library of Congress Cataloging-in-Publication Data
Craft of case-making and cabinet-making / G. Lister Sutcliffe,
    editor; Roy Underhill, consultant.
        p. cm.—(The Modern carpenter joiner and cabinet-maker)
    ISBN 0-918678-61-7
    1. Cabinet-work.   I. Sutcliffe, G. Lister.   II. Series.
TT197.C73 1990
684.1′6—dc20   90-6388
                                                   CIP

CONTENTS

DIVISIONAL-VOL. VII

SECTION IX.—STAIRS AND HANDRAILING (*Continued*)

BY GEORGE MILLER

SECTION X.—PART I.—AIRTIGHT CASE-MAKING

BY EDWARD B. BAKER

PART II.—WOOD-TURNING

BY R. W. COLE.

SECTION XI.—CABINET-MAKING
BY R. W. COLE

ILLUSTRATIONS

DIVISIONAL-VOL. VII

ILLUSTRATIONS IN TEXT

PREFACE

A few years before the publication of this series in 1906, novelist George Eliot penned *Adam Bede*, the classic romantic word-picture of the village joiner's shop, a place where: "The afternoon sun was warm on the five workmen there, busy upon doors and window-frames and wainscoting. . . . the slanting sunbeams shone through the transparent shavings that flew before the steady plane, and lit up the fine grain of the oak panelling which stood propped against the wall."

Eliot goes on to add dogs dozing on piles of shavings amid the honest, hearty workmen who sing aloud in the sunbeams. Surely life was better in those days before the trade unions sapped the vitality of the noble workman. But contrast Eliot's bucolic image with the descriptions of real London woodworking shops of the 1850s as recorded by social reformer Henry Mayhew. "The shop in which I work is for all the world like a prison—the silent system is as strictly carried out there as in a model gaol. If a man was to ask any common question of his neighbor, . . . he would be discharged there and then. If a journeyman makes the least mistake, he is packed off just the same."

No sunshine and singing here. Country carpenters from all over England traditionally went to London for a few years to refine their skill as "improvers." They then returned to their towns, taking with them the London styles and standards. But by the mid-nineteenth century, something had gone wrong, and countrymen increasingly fell into a web of murderous sweatshops that starved the workman and cheated the customer.

The emphasis on quality found in this volume was not of the least concern to the speculative developers mining gold in the growing demand for suburban London housing. The honest craftsmen were powerless against the laissez-faire culture of greed. Mayhew commented, "The public is being fleeced . . . to an extent that builders alone can know. . . . the houses are not safe to live in." Said one master builder, "Honesty is now almost impossible among us."

Skill and experience gained with age were no longer valued. The new masters wanted only the speed and strength of youth. Men were forced to conceal any indication of advancing age. "I used to wear glasses in one employ, and others did the same, and the foreman was a good man to the men as well as to the master; and if the master was coming, he used to sing out 'Take those sashes out of the way,' and so we had time to whip off our glasses, and the master didn't know we were forced to use them; but when he did find out, by coming into the shop unawares, he discharged two men."

Some of the loss of the value and dignity of these men's work and life was accounted to the introduction of steam-powered machinery. One of the house joiners interviewed by Mayhew recalled how mechanical planers gradually appropriated their work. At first the men welcomed the machines, as they did only the lowest level tasks, such as tonguing and grooving floorboards. "The joiners thought nothing at first of the planing of these boards by machinery, as only a certain class were put upon sash planing—it was beneath their dignity, and I have known men to leave a shop rather than do it." As the machines became more sophisticated though, they took over more complex and highly valued work, such as ornamental moldings, and displaced even the best of men.

Cabinetmaking did not escape the sweatshop shabbiness either. While some cabinetmakers remained in the "honorable" trade serving customers with a reasonable eye for quality, many labored in the "slaughter-houses" making cheap furniture for gullible people. "The deal's nailed together, and the veneer's dabbed on, and if the deal's covered, why the thing passes. The worst of it is that people don't understand either good work or good wood." Women and children were exploited as well. Women told Mayhew how they would stand at the bench with their young children polishing furniture from four in the morning until seven in the evening with no food, drink, or rest. Even with the husband fully employed, they could not earn enough to live on. This intolerable exploitation could not be sustaincd, and fcd thousands into the labor movements of the second half of the nineteenth century.

But by the end of the century, the anguish of those years was quickly forgotten by those who did not endure it. The truculence and swagger of the newly empowered union men engendered romantic nostalgia, and sermons such as we find here at the beginning of the chapter on cabinetmaking. "The only true way to success is that the heart be in the work; toiling not merely for the 'standard wage', nor creating a piece of work only to 'sell', but to last." True enough, but easier to say when your stomach is full and your children have a chance to outlive you.

ROY UNDERHILL
MASTER HOUSEWRIGHT
COLONIAL WILLIAMSBURG

E. *Newel.*—(1) Method of marking or setting off the mortises in newels to take string and handrail; (2) Mouldings of newel drawn on the wood for the turner; the parts with the diagonal lines show where the newel is to be kept square to receive the handrail and string; (3) Newel finished; the dotted lines indicate the tenons by which the handrail and string are fixed to the newel.

Plans of Stairs.—Before giving examples of the various forms of stairs ordinarily occurring in practice, we shall illustrate the mode of laying down the plan of a stair, where the height of the story, the number of the steps, and the space which they are to occupy are all given.

The first example shall be of the simplest kind, or dog-legged stairs.

Let the height (fig. 929) be 10 feet, the number of risers 17, the height of each riser consequently $7\frac{1}{17}$ inches, and the breadth of tread $9\frac{1}{2}$ inches; the width of the staircase 5 feet 8 inches. First lay down on the plan the width of the landing, then the size of the newel *a* in its proper position, the centre of the newel being on the riser line of the landing, which should be drawn at a distance from the back wall equal to the semi-width of the staircase, and at right angles to the side wall. Bisect the last riser of the lower flight at *o*, and describe an arc from the centre of the newel, as *o n*, on which set out the breadth of the winders; then to the centre of the newel, draw the lines indicating the face of each riser. If there be not space to get in the whole of the steps, winders may be also introduced on the left-hand side instead of the quarter-space shown.

The next example is a geometrical staircase.

Let A B C (fig. 930) be the plan of the walls where a geometrical stair is to be erected, and the line C be the line of the face of the first riser; let the whole height of the story be 11 feet

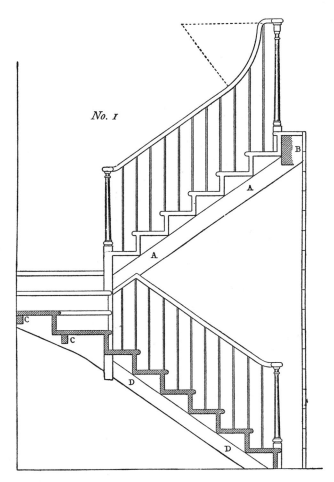

No. 1

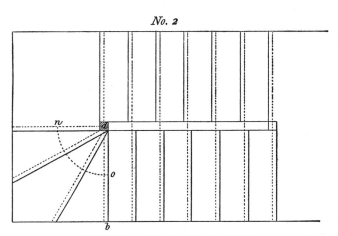

No. 2

Fig. 931.—Plan and Section of Dog-legged Stair

6 inches, and the height of riser 6 inches. The number of risers will consequently be twenty-three. The number of treads in each flight will be one fewer than the number of risers, so if there are two flights there will be twenty-one treads; or if winders are necessary, there will be twenty-two. Having first set out the opening of the well-hole, or the line of balusters, divide the width of the stairs into two equal parts, and continue the line of division

with a semicircle round the circular part, as shown by the dotted line in the figure; then divide this line from the first to the last riser into twenty-two equal parts, and if a proper width for each step can thus be obtained, draw the lines for the risers. This would, however, give a greater width of step than is required; take therefore 11 inches for the width of step,

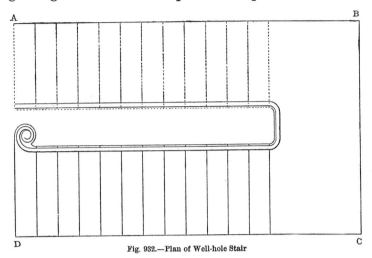

Fig. 932.—Plan of Well-hole Stair

and this, repeated twenty times, will reach to the line *d*, which is the last riser. There are in this case eight winders in the half-space, but four winders might be placed in one quarter-space; the other quarter-space might be made a landing, and additional fliers introduced, which would bring the last riser to the line A C. The usual place for the entrance to the cellar stairs is at D, but, allowing for the thickness of the carriages, the height obtainable there will be only about 6 feet, which is not sufficient. The point E in this example would be a better situation.

Nos. 1 and 2, fig. 931, show a section and plan of a dog-legged newel stair. The first quarter-space contains three winders, the next quarter-space is a landing; the lower flight is shown partly in section, exposing the rough string D D, and its connection

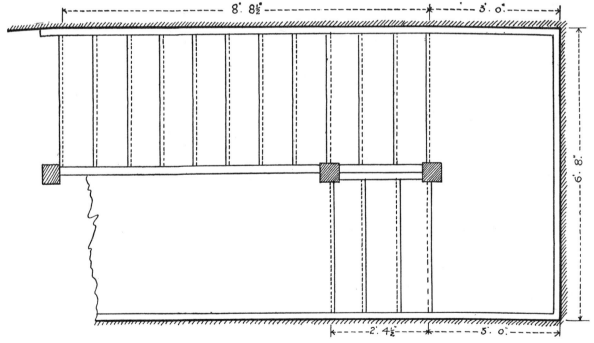

Fig. 933.—Plan of Two-flight Stair with Close Strings

with the bearers C C. The front string A A should be tenoned into the newels below and above.

Fig. 932 is the plan of a well-hole stair, with a landing in the half-space. The end of the well-hole is here composed of two circular quadrants connected by a straight line; this figure is not so graceful as the semicircle, but it allows more room on the landing.

TWO-FLIGHT STAIR WITH CLOSE STRING

This is a little more difficult than one having only a single flight. We will take, as an example, a stair to go into a space 6 feet 8 inches wide by 11 feet 8½ inches from start of riser to wall, with landings same width as stair, and close strings. The height from floor to upper landing is 9 feet 4 inches.

There must be a newel at the top of the first flight (that is, at the first landing), to receive the string of the first flight and the start of the upper string.

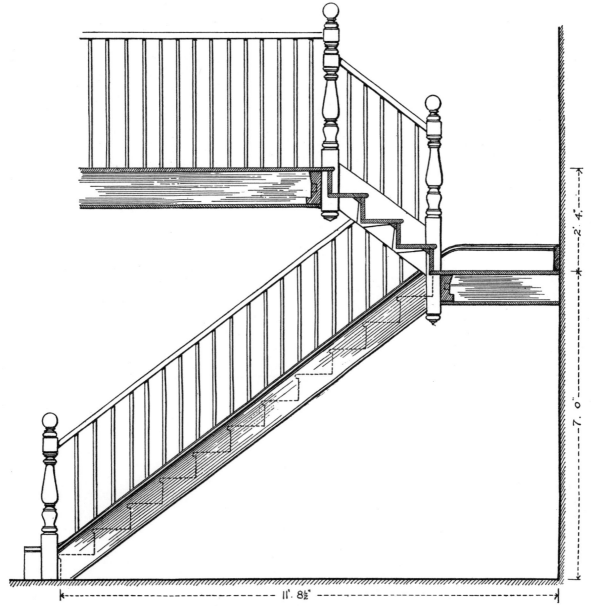

Fig. 934.—Section and Elevation of Two-flight Stair with Close Strings

In preparing the working drawings, proceed by laying down the plan as in fig. 933, marking off 11 feet 8½ inches from start of riser at front of stair to wall line at back, and also the going of stair for first flight 8 feet 8½ inches. At right angles to side of stair mark out the width between walls, 6 feet 8 inches, and divide this into the two widths of stair. Then mark off the width of landing and the going of next flight, 3 feet for landing and 2 feet 4½ inches for going of upper stair. The width of strings should now be drawn, and the position of newels.   Having done this, take the length of first going, which is 8 feet 8½ inches, and find the size and number of treads required, which will be 12 treads 9½ inches wide = 8 feet 8½ inches, and 3 treads 9½ inches wide for upper flight = 2 feet 4½ inches.

Next draw the elevation as shown in fig. 934, indicating the newels, joists, and landings, allowing ⅞ inch over trimmer joists for flooring, and the same underneath for ceiling boards or lath and plaster.   In the first place, measure off on the ground line 11 feet 8½ inches from wall line to start of first riser; then mark off on wall line the total height of stair, viz. 9 feet 4 inches, and 7 feet for height of first flight, which will leave 2 feet

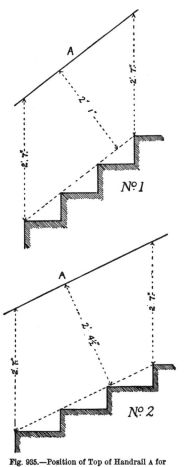

4 inches for second flight.   After this, mark the position of the trimmer with flooring and ceiling, as already explained, and then draw carefully the different newels.   The strings should now be drawn, and the treads and risers shown thereon, as explained in the description of the one-flight stair.

The height of the handrail is always taken on a line plumb with the riser, and measured from the top of the tread to the upper side of the handrail.   The body of a person going up or down a stair is naturally thrown slightly backwards or forwards, as the case may be, and 2 feet 7 inches has been found by experience to be the most suitable height.

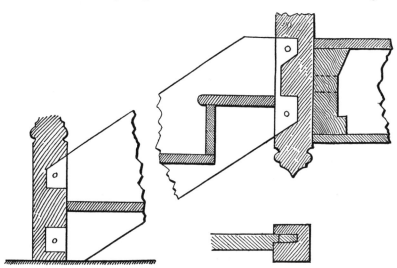

Fig. 935.—Position of Top of Handrail A for Steps of Different Sizes

Fig. 936.—String and Newels of Two-flight Stair with Close Strings

Fig. 935 shows the position of the handrail for steps of different widths; the heights 2 feet 7 inches are taken plumb from risers, but in No. 1 the distance at right angles from the line of nosing to the top of handrail is 2 feet 1 inch and in the other 2 feet 4½ inches, thus giving the most convenient place for the hand to rest on, which is slightly in advance of the body.

Now divide off the balusters, and draw the handrail on landing at the height of 3 feet 1 inch from floor to top of handrail.

The length of strings can now be taken, and the housings for treads, risers, and wedges marked on same by means of a pitch-board as explained in the stair of one flight with close string, allowing for the tenons at top and bottom, as shown by fig. 936.

The newels can now be set out; the squares to receive the handrail and strings on same must be very carefully marked.

Take the one at foot of stair, and mark it out as shown in the coloured plate.   Then the one at the intermediate landing, which will require a much longer square part at the bottom, as it must take the top part of the lower string and the bottom part of the upper string, and must have a drop moulding at the bottom. The top newel will require two square parts at the top to take the handrails of the upper flight and of the landing. The positions of the strings, handrails, and mortises should be drawn on the newels.

Sometimes the strings of a stair of this class are placed directly over each other, but it is much better to place them on each side of the centre line of the newel. This, of course, will throw the balusters to one side, but the difficulty can be got over by fixing outside the

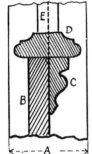

Fig. 937.—Section of Stair String and Hand-rail. A, Newel; B, string; C, moulding; D, capping; E, baluster; F, handrail

string B (fig. 937) a piece moulding C equal in thickness to the string, and nailing a cap D to the top of the string, wide enough at the top to take the balusters E, and at the bottom to cover the string and moulding. This method is the better, as it allows half of the handrail to be fixed to the return string.

In measuring off the wall string, the length must be taken from the ground-floor to the first landing, allowing the extra length at foot, beyond the line of newel, for the ease-ment or sweep between the string and skirting (fig. 938). The moulding down the upper edge of the wall string is worked inde-pendently and nailed on.

A very useful cupboard may be formed under the stair by fixing spandrel framing from the underside of outside string of lower flight to the floor level.

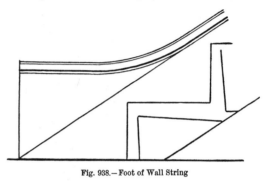

Fig. 938.—Foot of Wall String

Spandrels are formed in a number of ways, but the simplest is by nailing on ¾-inch match-boards and forming a door in same.

Handrails vary in form to suit the class of stair. Balusters are made from 1 inch to about 2 inches in thickness, and may be square, chamfered, pierced, or turned. As the balusters on landings are higher than those fixed on the top of close strings, the turned parts are usually higher, so that the square portions at the tops and bottoms of the two sets of balusters will be approximately equal.

CLOSE-STRING STAIR WITH WINDERS AT BOTTOM

When sizes are given for stairs, it is often found that the stair cannot be put in to give an easy step unless winders are introduced. In fig. 939 the space for the stair is 11 feet long and 2 feet 7 inches wide, and the rise 7 feet 3 inches, and a landing is required at the top 2 feet 7 inches broad with door opposite the top of stair.

Start by laying down the plan, 11 feet from wall to wall, 2 feet 7 inches for width of stair, and 2 feet 7 inches for landing, and as the stair must be 7 feet 3 inches high, find how many steps will be required, say, 12 risers at 7¼ inches = 7 feet 3 inches, therefore we shall have 11 treads; and as the space is limited, we introduce 3 winders at the bottom. The width of the winders, measured in the centre, should be, as nearly as possible, similar to the other treads.

As the space for foot-rest on the winders is narrowest round the newel, it is advisable to keep back the fliers from the newel and to draw the winders a little beyond the centre of newel, as shown in No. 1. No. 3 shows the wall string at foot of stair and the method of housing the treads and risers; No. 4 shows the grooves in bottom newel to receive treads and risers. A carriage-piece may be introduced under the centre of the stair to strengthen it, as shown in No. 5.

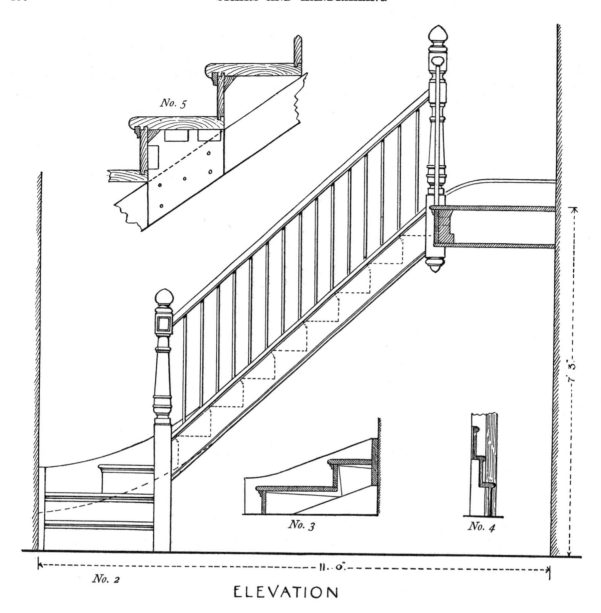

ELEVATION

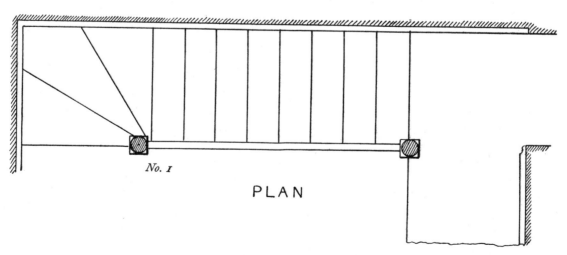

PLAN

Fig. 939.—Close-string Stair with Winders: No. 1, plan; No. 2, elevation; No. 3, wall-string at foot of stairs; No. 4, grooves in newel at foot of stairs
to receive winders; No. 5, section through steps showing middle carriage-piece and bracket

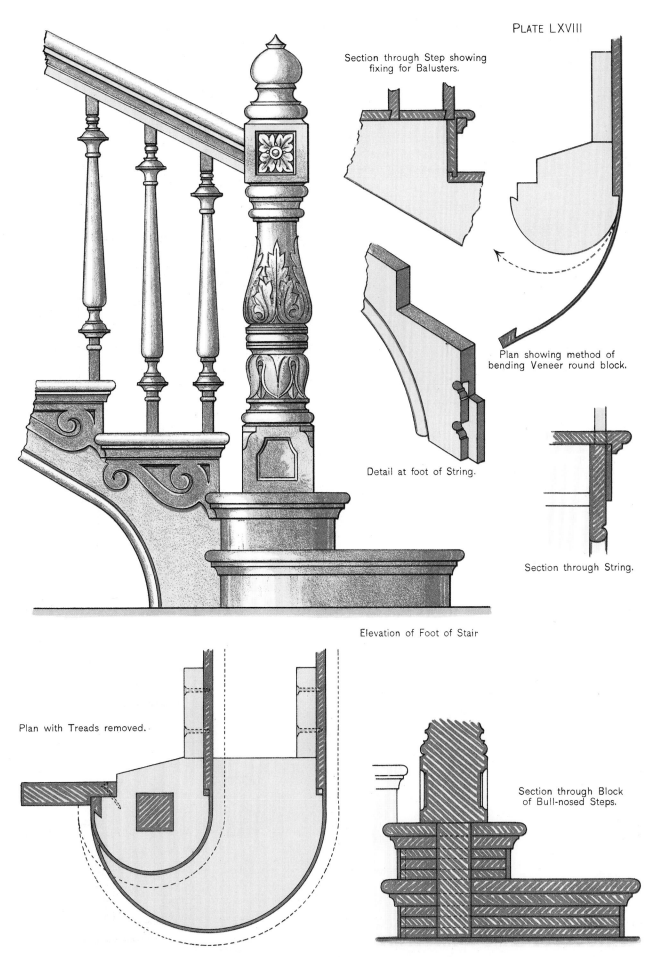

PLATE LXVIII

Section through Step showing
fixing for Balusters.

Plan showing method of
bending Veneer round block.

Detail at foot of String.

Section through String.

Elevation of Foot of Stair

Plan with Treads removed.

Section through Block
of Bull-nosed Steps.

OPEN-STRING STAIRS WITH BULL-NOSED STEPS AT FOOT

PLATE LXVIII

OPEN STRING STAIR WITH BULLNOSE STEPS AT THE BOTTOM

The principal figure in this plate is the side elevation of an open-string Stair with bull-nose steps at the bottom. The section near the top of the Newel shows the method of fixing Balusters to steps by means of dovetailed ends; below this is a view showing the lower end of the String and the manner in which it is prepared for fixing to blocks of Step. In the top corner is shown the plan of Step-block and method of bending the veneered part of Riser to same; underneath this is a section through the String showing the position of Bracket and projection of Tread over same.

The lower drawings on this plate are a plan and section of the bottom part of the Stair; the plan shows the blocks at the ends of the Steps with the veneered parts of the Risers going round them, also the position where the String is fixed to the blocks; the Tenon of the Newel is marked on the upper Step. The section shows the manner in which the blocks are built up and the Newel tenoned into them.

STAIR WITH OPEN OR CUT STRING

In an open-string stair the steps rest in angular notches formed by cutting away the upper edge of the outer string; the ends of the treads rest in these notches and project as far over the face of the string as the nosing does over the riser; the nosing is returned along the end of tread.

Fig. 940 is the plan of an open-string stair in two flights, 12 feet 8 inches from start of first flight to wall, 7 feet 2 inches from outer string to wall (viz. 3 feet over strings in each flight and 1 foot 2 inches between strings in well).

First draw the wall lines, and at 7 feet 2 inches from the side wall lay down the line of the outer string of first flight; then at 3 feet in from same draw the outer line of the inner

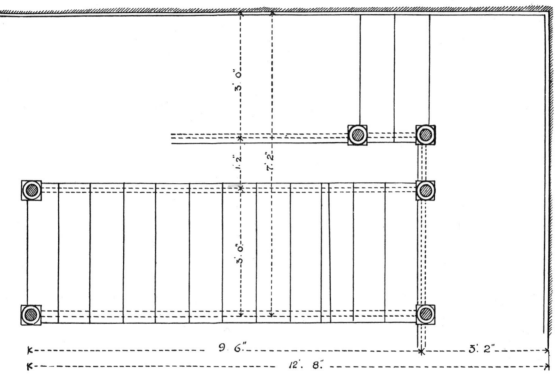

Fig. 940.—Plan of Stair with Open or Cut Strings

string. At 1 foot 2 inches from the last draw the line of the outer string of the upper flight and the trimmer of the landing. After this, mark the line of the intermediate landing 3 feet 2 inches from wall line, and draw lines for the thickness of the strings.

Find the number of steps required by taking the height to top landing, 9 feet 4 inches, and dividing by 16, which will give risers 7 inches high. Now find the width of treads by taking the going in first flight as 9 feet 6 inches, and divide same into 12 equal parts, which will give treads $9\frac{1}{2}$ inches wide. Draw these on the plan, and also the two treads of the upper flight, each $9\frac{1}{2}$ inches wide. After this carefully draw the positions of the different newels.

In drawing the elevation (fig. 941, No. 1), first put in the ground and wall lines, then from the wall mark off on the former 12 feet 8 inches to the start of first flight, and on the latter 9 feet 4 inches to top landing, and 7 feet 7 inches to intermediate landing. Draw the treads and risers: 12 treads at $9\frac{1}{2}$ inches for first going = 9 feet 6 inches, and 13 risers at 7 inches = 7 feet 7 inches; 2 treads for upper flight at $9\frac{1}{2}$ inches = 1 foot 7 inches, and 3 risers at 7 inches = 1 foot 9 inches. After this the newels must be carefully drawn; those at top of both flights will require two blocks at top, as they must take the handrails of stairs and landings. In laying down the lines of the handrails the heights are taken 2 feet 7 inches from front of step to top of handrail (see fig. 935) and 3 feet 1 inch on landings.

Great care must be taken in marking the position of strings and handrails on the newels; the square parts must be accurately shown, and the spaces required for turning

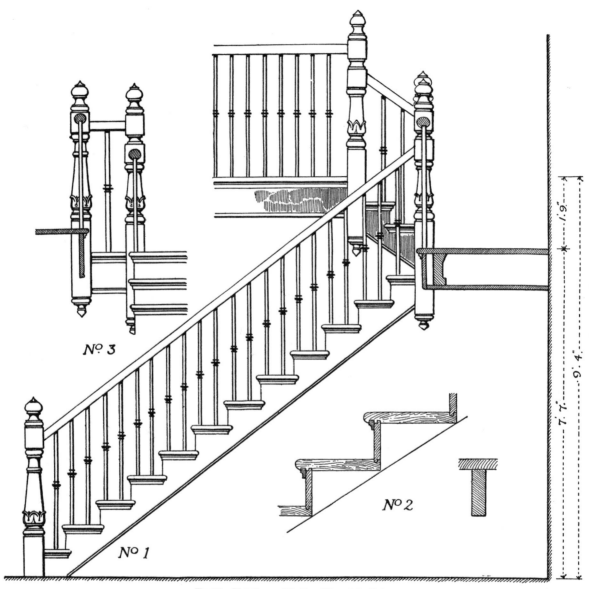

Fig. 941.—Elevations and Section of Open-string Stair

(see coloured plate). Two balusters are shown on each tread, and the same spacing is adopted as nearly as possible on the landings.

Angular carriage-pieces are fixed in the centre below the treads and behind the risers to strengthen the stairs (fig. 941, No. 2).

The principal figure in Plate LXVIII is the side elevation of an open-string stair with bull-nose steps at the bottom. The section near the top of the newel shows the method of fixing balusters to steps by means of dovetailed ends; below this is a view showing the lower end of the string and the manner in which it is prepared for fixing to blocks of step. In the top corner is shown the plan of step-block and method of bending the veneered part of riser to same; underneath this is a section through the string showing the position of bracket and projection of tread over same.

The lower drawings on this plate are a plan and section of the bottom part of the stair; the plan shows the blocks at the ends of the steps with the veneered parts of the risers going round them, also the position where the string is fixed to the blocks; the tenon of the newel is marked on the upper step. The section shows the manner in which the blocks are built up and the newel tenoned into them.

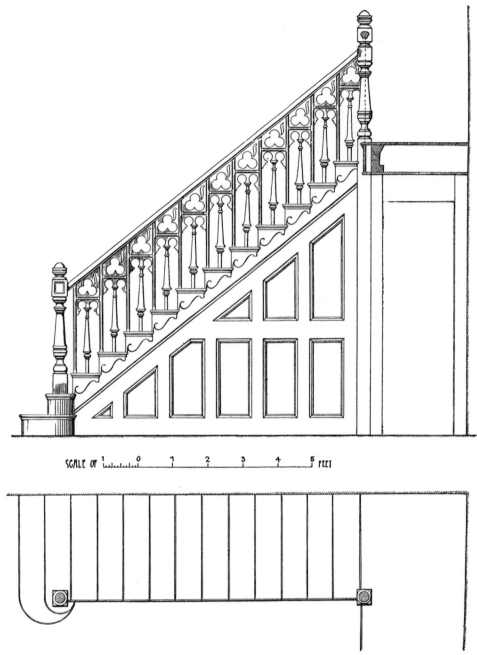

SCALE OF 0 1 2 3 4 5 FEET

Fig. 942.—Plan and Elevation of Open-string Stair with Bull-nose Step

OPEN-STRING STAIR WITH BULL-NOSE STEP

The method of drawing is similar to that explained for other stairs. This example (fig. 942) shows an open or cut string with brackets. These are usually about $\frac{3}{8}$-inch thick, and are fixed under the treads which project over the face of the string and finish flush with the brackets.

Fig. 943 shows the detail of outside of step and method of fixing the return moulding. The holes in the tread for balusters are also shown, and are marked off on the end of the treads by a template, as in fig. 944. The template (No. 1) may be made out of a piece of stuff about 15 inches × 2 inches × $\frac{3}{8}$ inch, to which are nailed the two templates for the baluster dovetails, and the one for marking the part to be cut away for the string.

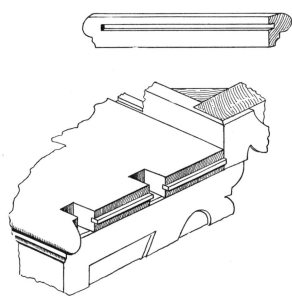

Fig. 943.—Detail of Return-moulding and End of Tread

No. 2 is the plan of the end of the tread, and No. 3 shows the method of applying the template to the tread.

The panelled part under the string is called a spandrel, and a door is often formed in it so that the space under the stairs may be used as a press. The framing is usually made out of stuff $1\frac{1}{4}$ inch thick, the middle and bottom rails 9 inches wide, and the top rail, stile, and muntins or mullions $4\frac{1}{2}$ inches wide. The framing is put together like a door, with mortises and tenons.

Bull-nose steps are usually built up by a three-piece block as in No. 1 (fig. 945), which is a section through the step indicating the blocks, tread, and bearer of riser. No. 2 is a plan showing the veneer of the riser before being bent into position. The small cross-hatched part at the end of the tread and the start of the veneer is the wedge for tightening up the latter. Nos. 3 and 4 show alternate methods of forming bull-nose steps. For other details see Plate LXVIII and fig. 975.

To ensure a good fixing for the newel, it is advisable to make a square hole through both blocks of the bottom steps, great care being taken to have them plumb. The newel should be shouldered and tenoned, and glued into the mortise of the steps, and may also be fixed by screws from the back of the blocks.

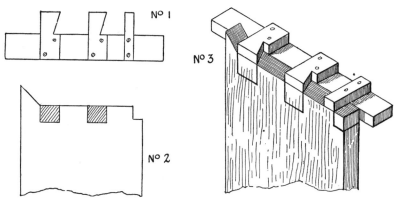

Fig. 944.—Template for Dovetails of Balusters, &c., and Method of Application

No. 1, fig. 946, shows the plan of a geometrical stair with winders. In the first quarter-space, or lower half of the figure, the lines of the steps are drawn to the centre of the well-hole, and this is the usual way of placing the risers; but drawn thus as radii of the circle, they are, obviously, too narrow at the inner end next the well-hole, and too wide next the wall, and if two persons were passing each other they would both be forced to use the parts of the tread most inconvenient to walk upon. Further, as the risers of the steps are all of equal height, it follows that the slope or ramp of the string board along the end of the fliers, from the first to the seventh step, will be much less steep than that which subtends the narrow end of the winders, and the result will be a very ungraceful knee at their junction. Both of these inconveniences can be overcome by adjusting the steps in such a way as to distribute the inequality amongst them, or as the French term it, by making the steps dance, as is shown in the upper half of the figure. This may be accomplished either by calculation or graphically. By the first method, the step in the centre of the circular arc is regarded as a fixed line and the divergence from parallelism has to be made between it and the extremes either way. But it is not necessary to begin the divergence at the first and last steps, nor indeed is it advisable, and in general the first and last three or four steps are left unaltered, so that they may be perfectly parallel to the landing. Suppose, then, that the divergence is fixed to commence at the fourth step, it becomes necessary to distribute eight spaces along the centre of the string, commencing at the central riser No. 12, which, from this riser to the fourth, shall follow some law of uniform progression, say that of arithmetical progression, as being the most simple. The progression then will consist of eight terms, the sum of which shall be equal to the length from the twelfth to the fourth step. Suppose that its development is 66 inches, a length composed of the breadth of three fliers, 4 to 6, namely 36 inches, and the sum of the widths of the ends of the five winding steps, 7 to 11, namely 30 inches,

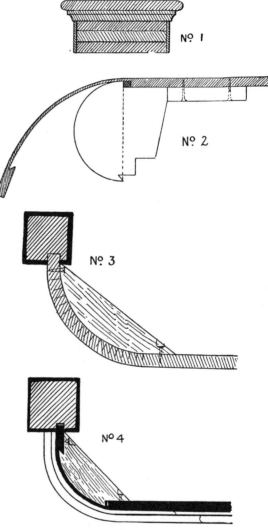

Fig. 945.—Three Methods of constructing Bull-nose Steps

Subtracting from ...   ...   66 inches
The width of the eight steps of
    the same width as the winders   48   „

There is obtained the difference   18   „

from which is to be furnished the progressive increase to the steps as they proceed from the centre to riser No. 4. Suppose these increments to follow the law of the natural numbers 1 2 3 4 5 6 7 8, the sum of which is 36, divide the difference 18 by 36, and the quotient, 0·5 inch, is the first line of the progression, and the steps will increase as follows:—

The end of step No. 11	= $6\frac{1}{2}$		The end of step No. 7	= $8\frac{1}{2}$
„ 10	= 7		„ 6	= 9
„ 9	= $7\frac{1}{2}$		„ 5	= $9\frac{1}{2}$
„ 8	= 8		„ 4	= 10

The sum of which is 66 inches.

These widths, taken from a scale, are to be set off on the line of balusters, and from the points so obtained, lines are to be drawn through the divisions of the centre line, these latter divisions being all equal. It is easy to perceive that by this method, and by varying the progression, any form may be given to the curve of the string.

The graphic method, however, is preferable, as it is important to give a graceful curve to the development of the string.

Let the dotted line *s m p*, No. 2, represent the kneed line made by the first division of the stairs in the lower part *s m*, corresponding to the nosing of the fliers, and the upper part *m p* to that of the winders. On *m n* at the point *p* raise a perpendicular *p i*. Then set off *m s* equal to *m p*, and make *s r* perpendicular to *s m*. The intersection of these two perpendiculars, *s r* and *p i*, gives the centre of the arc of a circle, tangential in *s* and *p* to the sides of the angle *s m p*. In like manner is found the arc to which *p n*, *n o* are tangents, and a species of cyma is formed by the two arcs, which is a graceful double-curve line without knees.

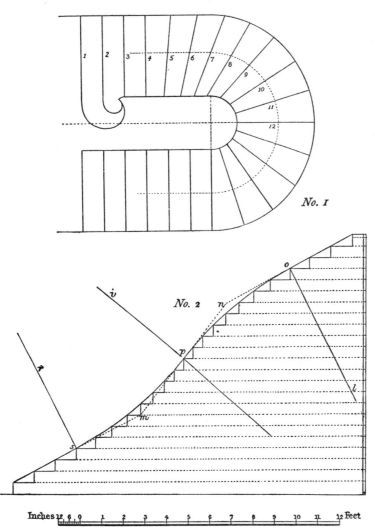

This line is met by the horizontal lines, which indicate the surface of the treads, the point *p* being always the fixed point of the centre step, the twelfth in this example. Therefore the heights of the risers are drawn from the story rod to meet the curved line of development, *s p o*, and are thence transferred to the baluster line on a plan.

Plate LXIX. fig. 1.—Nos. 1 and 2 are the plan and elevation of a geometrical stair, composed of straight flights, with quarter-space landings, and rising 15 feet 9 inches.

The first flight is shown in fig. 1, No. 2, partly in section, exhibiting the carriage *c c*, T the trimmer for the quarter-space, and v the trimmer of the floor below, with the lower end of iron baluster fastened by a screw and nut *d*, at the under side of the trimmer v.

Fig. 2.—No. 1 exhibits the plan, and No. 2 the elevation of a geometrical stair, with straight flights connected by winders on the quarter-spaces.

Fig. 946.—Plan and Development of String of Geometrical Stair

Plate LXX contains illustrations of stairs for a chapel, designed by the editor. The staircase is square, and the stairs are arranged around a central well with newels at the angles. The stairs and balusters are of oak, and the handrails and newels of walnut. The newels at the corners of the two lowest quarter-space landings are carried down to the floor, and the spandrels filled with panelling. The other newels have moulded drops. The newels are square, this form of section being better adapted for receiving the strings and handrails than a round section. The newel at the foot of the stairs is larger and more elaborate than the others.

Plate LXXI.—Fig. 1 is a plan, and fig. 3 a side elevation of a geometrical stair, with a half-space of winders. The positions of the rough strings or carriages are shown on the plan by dotted lines, *e g*, *e f*, *h i*, *f k*. This is a simpler mode of forming the carriages of stairs than that generally practised; having fewer joints, it is also stronger. It is fully illustrated and described as applied to the more intricate example of elliptical stairs in Plate LXXII.

PLATE LXIX

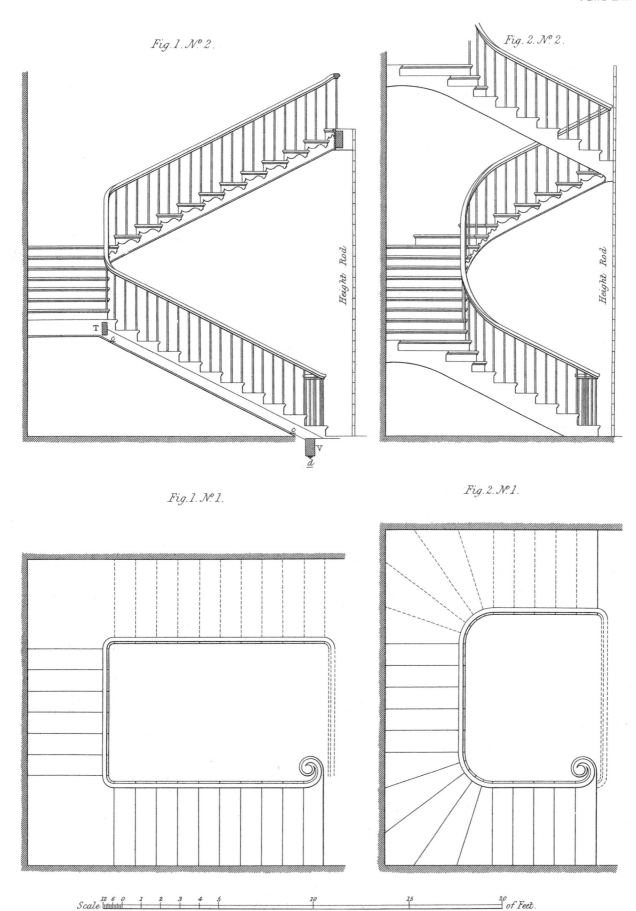

Fig. 1. N.º 2.

Fig. 2. N.º 2.

Height Rod.

Height Rod.

T
c
c
V
d

Fig. 1. N.º 1.

Fig. 2. N.º 1.

Scale 12 6 0   1   2   3   4   5   10   15   20   of Feet.

PLANS AND ELEVATIONS OF GEOMETRICAL STAIRS

PLATE LXX

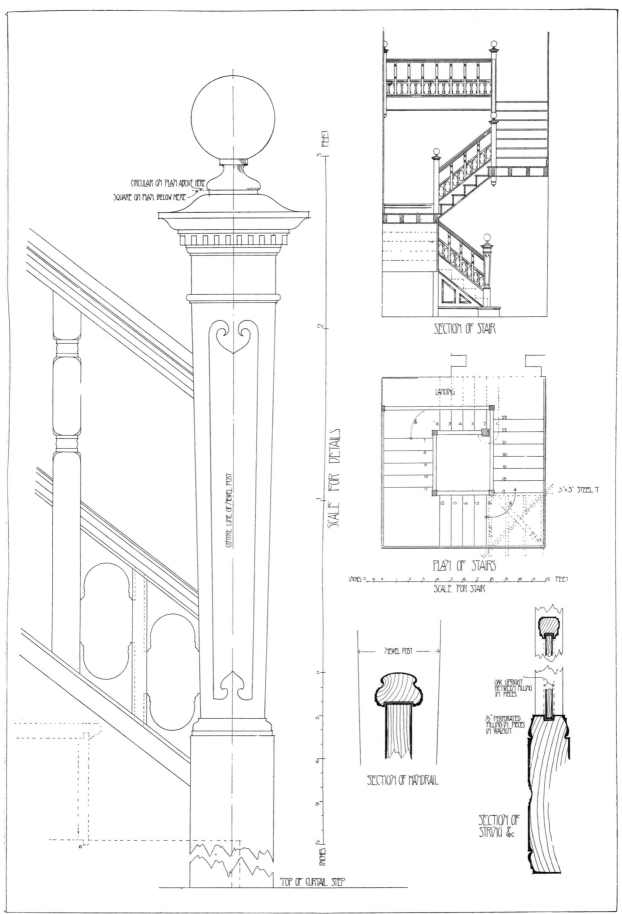

CIRCULAR ON PLAN ABOVE HERE

SQUARE ON PLAN BELOW HERE

CENTRE LINE OF NEWEL POST

SCALE FOR DETAILS

TOP OF CURTAIL STEP

SECTION OF STAIR

LANDING

3"x3" STEEL T

PLAN OF STAIRS

SCALE FOR STAIR

NEWEL POST

SECTION OF HANDRAIL

OAK UPRIGHT BETWEEN FILLING IN PIECES

½" PERFORATED FILLING-IN PIECES IN WALNUT

SECTION OF STRING &c.

Sutcliffe & Sutcliffe, Architects

OPEN-WELL STAIRS, BIRCHCLIFFE CHAPEL

Fig. 2 shows the plan, and fig. 4 the end elevation of a geometrical stair with part winders and part landing, well adapted for a situation where a door has to be entered from the landing. The line A B on the plan shows the situation where the principal carriage should be introduced.

Plate LXXII exhibits a plan (fig. 1, No. 1) and elevation (figs. 1 and 2) of an elliptical stair with winders throughout. Fig. 2 is an elevation of the stair from the ground floor

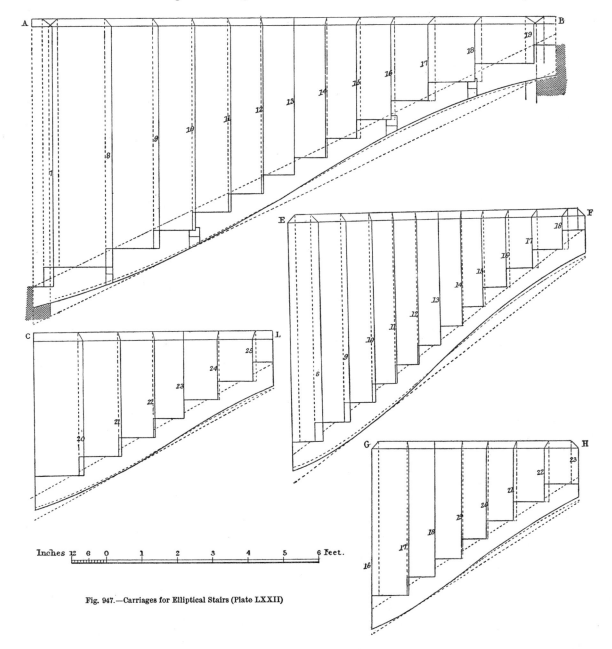

Fig. 947.—Carriages for Elliptical Stairs (Plate LXXII)

to the first floor, and fig. 1 an elevation of the balustrade along the first floor landing, and of part of the stair from the first to the second floor. On the plan the carriages are shown by dotted lines. These carriages are delineated in plan and elevation in fig. 947.

No. 1 is the longest carriage or rough string, A B, and is formed of one deal 11 inches wide by 3 or 4 in thickness; its length of bearing between the walls is about 15 feet. To find the best position for the carriages, lay a straight-edge on the plan, and by its application find where a right line will be divided into nearly equal parts by the intersection of the risers. The object of this will readily be understood, if it is considered that in a series of steps of *equal* width and risers of equal height, the angles will be in a straight line, whereas in a series of *unequal* steps and *equal* risers, the angles will deviate from a straight line in proportion to the inequality in the width of the steps. It seldom happens that carriages cannot be applied to stairs, if their situation is carefully selected by the means above-mentioned. The double line A B is taken from the plan (fig. 1, No. 1, Plate LXXII), with the lines of the risers crossing at various angles of inclination. These lines represent the back surface of each riser, according to the number on each. The double line A B will therefore be understood as representing the thickness of the piece. Lines drawn from the intersections of each of the risers perpendicularly on A B will present the width of bevel which each notching will require in the carriage. The complete lines show the side of the carriage nearest the well-hole, whilst the dotted

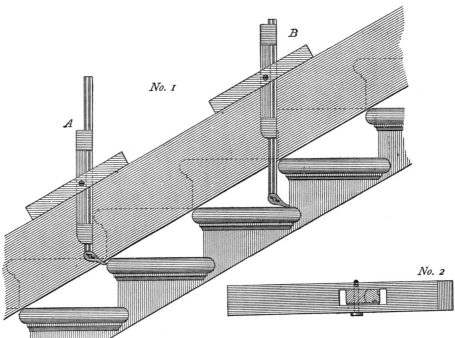

Fig. 948.—Method of Scribing Skirting on Stairs

lines represent the side nearest the wall. The most expeditious method of setting out such carriages is to draw them full size on a floor. Having first set out the plan of the stairs, take off the width of every step in the order in which it occurs, marking that width, and at right angles thereto draw the connecting riser, thus proceeding step by step till the whole length of the carriage is completed; next set out one side of the carriage as a face side, and square over to the back, allowing the bevel as found on the plan; then, with a pair of compasses, prick off to the under edge at each angle for the strength; this will define the curvature for the under side with its proper wind, to suit the ceiling surface of the stairs. The bearer, C D, fig. 1, No. 1, Plate LXXII, is a level piece wedged in the wall, with its square end abutting against the side of the carriage, A B. The straight dotted lines in the elevation of the carriage, No. 1, fig. 947, are intended to show the edges of an 11-inch deal previous to its being cut; the shaded part at each end shows its bearing in the wall; at the riser 18 is shown a corpsing, to receive the lower end of the carriage, C L (No. 3); and at the riser 16, a similar corpsing to receive the carriage, G H (No. 4); No. 2 is the carriage, E F, parallel with A B, and the front string is nailed against it.

Plate LXXIII exhibits a stair winding round a large cylindrical newel. Fig. 1 is the plan, and fig. 2 the elevation. The lower part of the newel is composed of cylindrical

PLATE LXXI

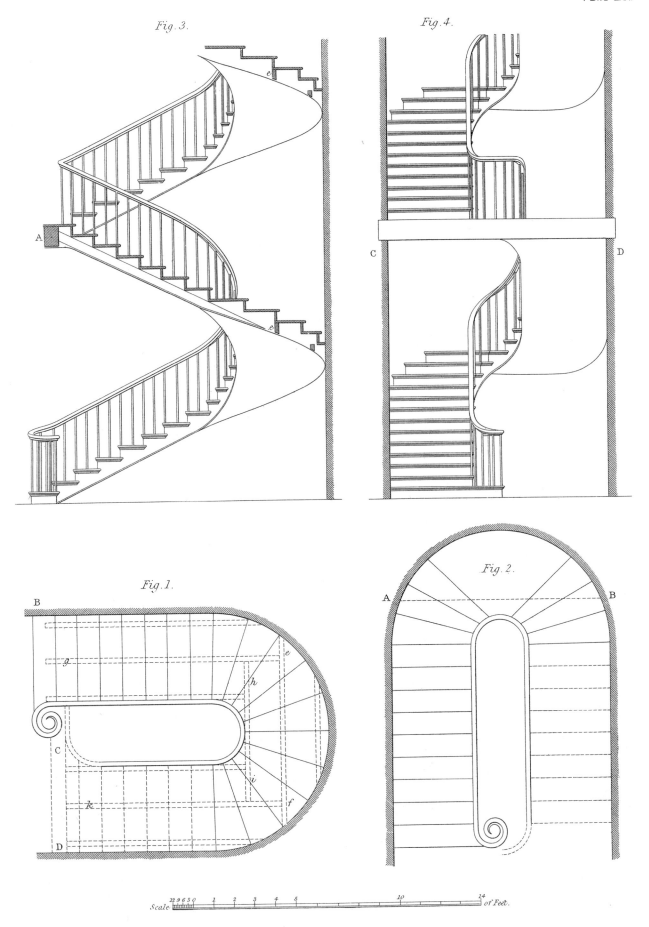

Fig. 3.

Fig. 4.

Fig. 1.

Fig. 2.

Scale 12 9 6 3 0   1   2   3   4   5   10   14 of Feet.

PLANS AND ELEVATIONS OF GEOMETRICAL STAIRS

PLATE LXXII

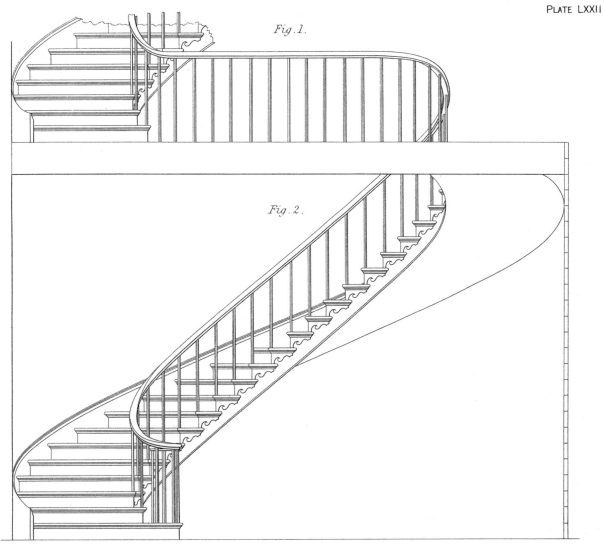

Fig. 1.

Fig. 2.

Fig. 1. N°. 1.

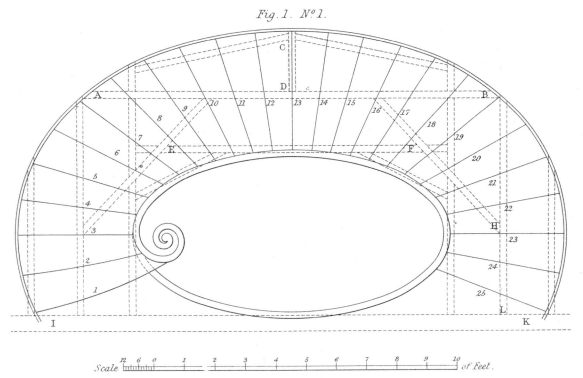

Scale of Feet.

GEOMETRICAL STAIRS—ELLIPTICAL PLAN

staving of 2-inch plank, into which the risers and bearers to each step are fixed, the detail of which is better seen in fig. 4, drawn to a larger scale. The manner in which the steps and risers are put together is shown in fig. 3; the risers are grooved, and the steps tongued into them. This figure shows the ends of the steps before the last thin casing of string-board is fixed. They are united by a band of iron screwed to the bearers throughout the entire length.

Method of Scribing the Skirting. — Fig. 948 shows the method of scribing skirting on stairs. The instrument used for this purpose is shown in two positions, A and B, No. 1. It is something like a bevel in form, but has a slider with a steel point at the end; this slider moves steadily in collars, so that while the steel point rests on any point on the stairs, another point on the slide denotes on the skirting-board the corresponding point, thus remedying a defect of the common compasses by maintaining always

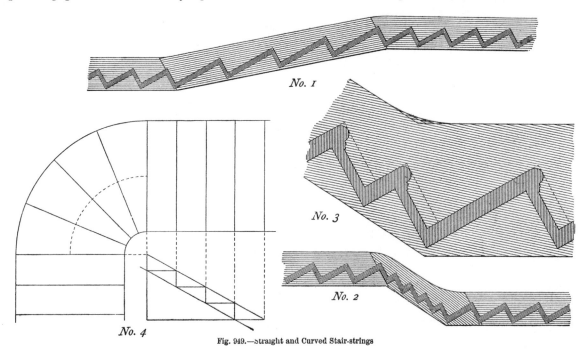

No. 1

No. 3

No. 2

No. 4

Fig. 949.—Straight and Curved Stair-strings

a parallel motion. No. 2 is another view of the same instrument, showing the mortise in which the slide works.

Strings. — Nos. 1 to 3, fig. 949, show portions of a string-board for the steps shown in plan in No. 4; the middle part of No. 1 is a flexible veneer intended to be bent on a cylinder of a suitable curvature, and blocked on the back by pieces in a perpendicular position. No. 2 is the string-board in development for the smaller end of the winders, and No. 3 a more enlarged view of the same, showing the mode of easing the angle by intersecting lines.

In circular strings, the string-board for the circular part is prepared in several different ways. Each of these will now be described, the first being that adopted in *veneered strings.*

One indispensable requisite in forming a veneered string is called by joiners a *cylinder*; it is, however, in fact, a semi-cylinder joined to two parallel sides. An apparatus of this kind must first be formed of a diameter equal to the distance betwixt the faces of the strings in the stairs.

Take some flexible material, such as a slip of paper, and measure the exact stretch-out of the circular part of the cylinder, from the springing line on one side to the springing line on the other. Lay out this as a straight line on a drawing-board; then examine the plan of the stairs, and measure therefrom the precise place of each riser coming in contact with or near to the circular part of the well-hole as it intersects on the line of the face of the string, and also the distance of such riser from the springing lines. These distances should all be carefully marked on the slip of paper, and transferred to the drawing-board; then, with the pitch-board, set out the development of the line of steps, by making each step equal to the width found, and .connecting with it at right angles its proper height of riser. When the whole development has been set out on the drawing-board, mark from the angles of the steps downwards the dimension for the strength of carriage; by this means it will be seen what shape and size of veneer will be required. The whole of the setting out must now be transferred to the face of the veneer; then with the point of an awl prick through the angles of the steps and risers, and trace the lines on the back as well as on the front. The veneer must now be bent down on the cylinder, bringing the springing lines and centre lines of the string to coincide as exactly as possible with those of the cylinder; the whole string must then be carefully backed by staving-pieces glued on it, with the joints and grain parallel to the axis of the cylinder. The manner of jointing the staves is shown in fig. 950, where a bevel is set with the

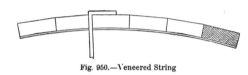

Fig. 950.—Veneered String

tongue in the line of the radius, whilst the stock coincides with the back of the stave. The lines on the back of the string will serve to indicate the quantity of the veneer to be covered by the staving. The whole must be allowed to remain on the cylinder till sufficiently dry and firm. It is next fitted to the work, by cutting away all the superfluous wood as directed by the lines on the face of the veneer, and then being perfectly fitted to the steps, risers, and connecting string, it must be firmly nailed both to the steps and risers, and also to the carriages. Each heading joint in the string should be grooved and tongued with a glued tongue.

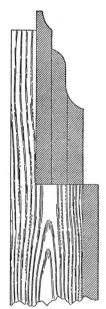

Fig. 951.
String-board for Elliptical
Stairs (Plate LXXII)

Another method of gluing up the strings is sometimes practised. In this the string is set out as before described, but instead of using a thin veneer, an inch board is taken, on the face of which the development of steps, risers, springing and centre lines must be carefully set out as before. The edge of the board must be gauged from the face, equal to the thickness of a veneer, which would bind round the cylinder; the string must then be confined down on the work-bench, and grooves made by a dado grooving-plane on its back in the direction of the riser, and at about half an inch distant from each other, till the whole width of the cylindric surface is formed into a regular succession of grooves and projections; the string must then be bent on the cylinder, and the grooves filled with small bars of wood, carefully glued in. When dry, this is to be fitted to the stairs, as in the former method.

Another method is, making staves hollowed on the face to the curvature of the well-hole, and setting out as much of the string on each piece as will cover its width, then gluing the staves, edge to edge, without any veneer. This method, though expeditious, is not safe.

A fourth method is sometimes practised, when the curved surface is of great length and large sweep, as in the back strings of circular stairs. In this a portion of the cylindric surface is formed on a solid plank template, about 3 or 4 feet in length; and a veneer of board sufficiently thin to bend easily is laid down round the curve, and a number of pieces of like thickness are added in succession to make the required thickness of the string-board. In working this method, the glue is introduced between the veneers with a thin piece of wood, and the veneers quickly strained down to the curved piece with hand-screws. A string can be

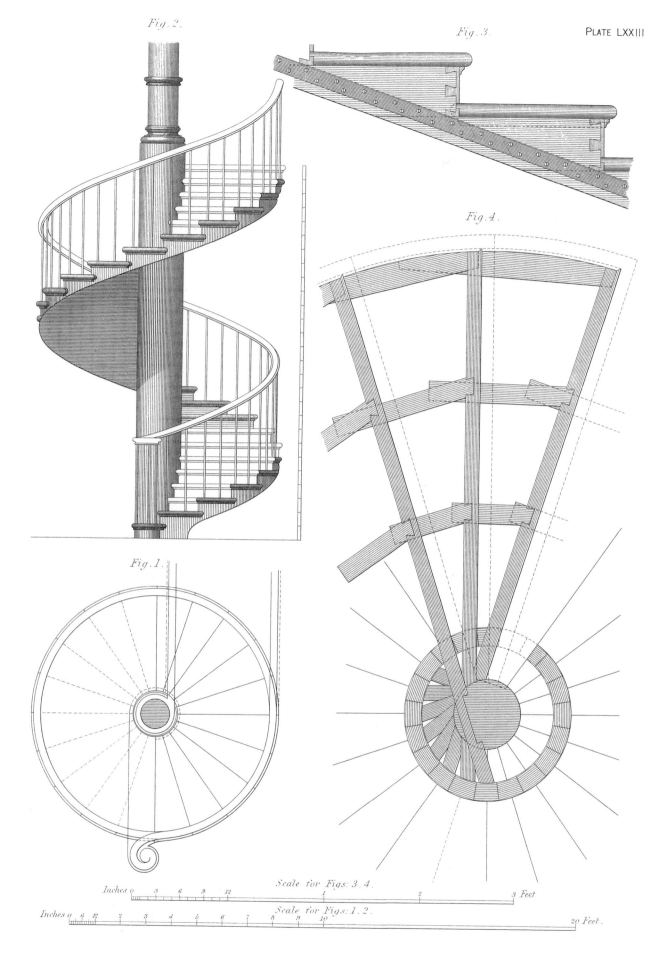

PLATE LXXIII

Fig. 2.

Fig. 3.

Fig. 4.

Fig. 1.

Scale for Figs: 3.4.

Inches 0   3   6   9   12   1   2   3 Feet

Scale for Figs: 1.2.

Inches 0 6 12   2   3   4   5   6   7   8   9   10   20 Feet

CIRCULAR STAIRS

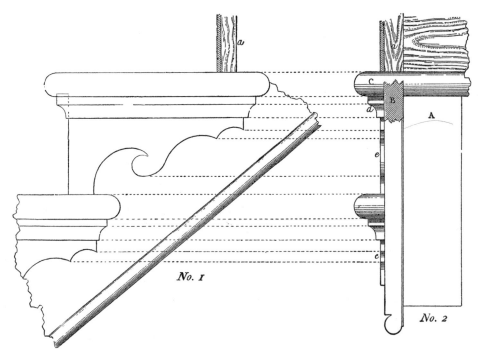

Fig. 952.—Stair-brackets, &c

formed in this way to almost any length by gluing a few feet at a time, and when that dries, removing the cylindric curve and gluing down more, till the whole is completed.

Fig. 951 shows how a back string is formed for the stair in Plate LXXII, with a base moulding formed in thicknesses, and applied to the string.

Brackets.—Fig. 952, No. 1, shows a portion of front string with bracket, and the mitred end of a riser at *a*. No. 2 shows the back of the same riser, and how it is shouldered and mitred to receive the front string and bracket; B shows the thickness of the front string, A the carriage, C the thickness of the tread, *d* the hollow, and *e* the end of the bracket.

To diminish the bracket of the fliers to suit the winders, make one of the fliers, marked B, fig. 953, the base of a right-angled triangle, B D C, setting off any convenient distance, B C, for the perpendicular. Lay down E A, the length of the shorter bracket required to be drawn, parallel to D B; draw ordinates through each member of the original bracket, and through the points of their intersection with B D, draw lines converging to the point C. The intersection of these with the line A will divide it for the corresponding set of ordinate lines, which draw, and make equal respectively to those on the line B; trace the contour through the various points thus obtained, and the bracket A will be produced. To enlarge a bracket, it is only necessary to

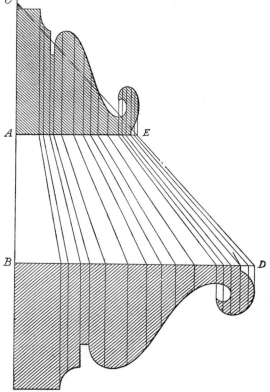

Fig. 953.—Method of enlarging and diminishing Stair-brackets

reverse the process by making the shorter bracket, as A, the base of the triangle, producing from it the perpendicular and hypotenuse.

CHAPTER II

HANDRAILING

The *horizontal,* or *ground plane,* is that plane on which the plan is drawn.

The *vertical plane* is any plane considered as standing perpendicular on the ground plane.

The *oblique plane, cutting plane,* or *plane of the plank* is that plane on which the mould of the rail is produced.

The *trace* of any plane is a line forming the termination of one plane and its junction with another; thus the angle of a block of marble is the *trace* of the plane of any one of its sides on another side which it meets. The *trace* therefore is a line, and the only line which can be drawn common to either of two planes meeting each other at an angle.

A *cylinder* is a solid, described by geometricians as generated by the rotation of a rectangle about one of its sides, supposed to be at rest; this quiescent side is called the *axis* of the *cylinder*; the base and top of the cylinder are equal or similar circles.

A *prism* is a solid, whose base and top are similar right-line figures, with sides formed in planes, and rising perpendicularly from the base to the top.

The *cylinder,* so called by *joiners,* is a solid figure, compounded of the two last-mentioned figures; its base is composed of a *semicircle* joined to a *right-angled parallelogram.* This last compound figure is intended whenever the word *cylinder* occurs in the following article, unless the word *geometrical* be prefixed.

HEIGHT OF HANDRAILS.—The height of the handrail of a stair need not be uniform throughout, but may be varied within the limits of a few inches, so as to secure a graceful line at the changes of direction. The rail may also with propriety be made higher at the landings, the position of the body being then erect, than at the sloping part. The height of the rail on the straight part of the stairs should be about 2 feet 7 inches, measured vertically from the nosing of the tread to the upper side of the rail; to this there should be added at the landings not less than the height of half a riser.

In winding stairs, regard should be had, in adjusting the height of the rail, to the position of a person using it who may be thrown farther from it at some points than at others, not only by the narrowing of the treads, but by the oblique position of the risers. Take, for example, the elliptical stairs (Fig. 1, No. 1, Plate LXXII), and suppose the rails of uniform height. A person in ascending, with the foot on the nosing of steps 6 or 7, will find the rail lower to the hand than when standing on the nosings of 19 and 20. The risers of steps 3, 13, and 23 are square with the rail, while those of the other steps are more or less oblique. In such a case it is advisable, to make the rail of the average height over 3, 13, and 23, to raise it several inches higher at 7, and to depress it to an equal extent over 19 and 20; to raise it, also, at the top of the stairs, the more especially as the easing of the rail will tend to lower it there. It is seldom that the rail will require to be lowered below the assumed standard more than 3 inches, or raised above it more than 4 inches, and unless these variations in the height are adjusted in accordance with the foregoing considerations, the effect will be very disagreeable.

It is necessary to guard the reader against the common error of raising the rail over winders, especially such as are of steep pitch. The height should be uniform, except in the instances adduced above.

WREATHS.—*Construction of Wreath when the Ground-Plan is a Quarter-Circle and its Pitches Equal* (fig. 954).—Draw the Quarter-Circle A B C on ground plan, then draw the line

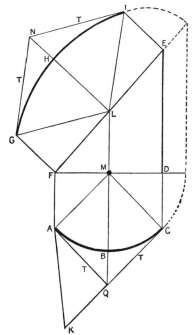

Fig. 954.—Wreath with Quarter-Circle Plan and equal Pitches

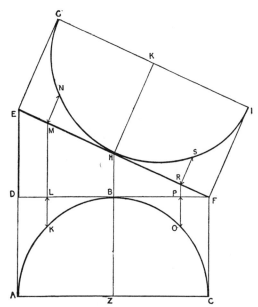

Fig. 955.—Wreath with Semicircular Plan

F D, and at right angles to the same draw A F, B L, and C D E, and on C D E set off the height D E and join E F, cutting B L at L. From the points F, L, and E erect the perpendiculars F G, L H, and E I, making them equal to F A, M B, and D C respectively. An arc drawn through the points G, H, and I, will be the line required. To find the tangents, draw C Q and A Q at right angles to M C and M A; to find the tangents on the cut line, produce L H to N, making L N equal to M Q, and draw G N and N I, which are the tangent lines required. In the illustration, A B C is the plan, D E the height, A K Q the pitch-board, T T the tangents, and G H I L the section through the cut-line E F.

Wreath when the Ground-Plan is a Half-Circle (fig. 955).—Let A B C be the ground-plan described from the centre Z. Draw A D, Z B, and C F perpendicular to A C, and through B draw D F parallel to A C. Produce A D to E, making D E equal to the height required. Join E F, which is the line of the cut through the cylinder, and on the same erect the perpendiculars E G, H K, and F I, equal to A D, Z B, and C F, and draw the line G K I. Divide A B and B C on the ground-plan into two equal parts at K and O, and erect the lines K L M and O P R perpendicular to D F to meet F E in M and R, and from these points draw M N and R S perpendicular to E F and equal to L K and O P. A line drawn through the points G, N, H, S, I gives the line required, *i.e.* the section on the cut-line. Any number of points in the curve can be found in a similar manner.

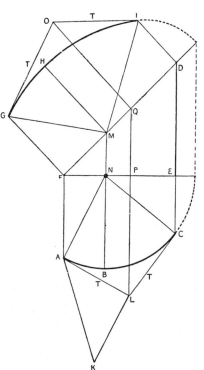

Fig. 956.—Wreath with Plan less than a Quarter-Circle

Wreath with Ground-Plan less than a Quarter-Circle (fig. 956).—Let A B C be the given arc, which is less than a quarter-circle. Through the centre N draw F E, and from C draw

C D perpendicular to F E, making E D equal to the height required. From A and B draw A F and B N perpendicular to F E, and join D F by a line cutting B N produced in M. From F, M, and D erect the lines F G, M H, and D I perpendicular to the cut-line D F and equal to F A, N B, and E C respectively. The points G, H, I will be in the line required.

The tangent A L is at right angles to N A, and the tangent L C to N C. To find the tangents for the cut-line, draw L P perpendicular to F E and produce till it cuts D F in the point Q; from Q draw Q O perpendicular to D F and equal to P L; I O and G O are the tangents on the cut-line. A K L is the pitch-board.

Wreath with Ground-Plan more than a Quarter-Circle and Pitches Unequal (fig. 957)—Let A B C be the given plan and E D the height. The method of construction is exactly the same as in the preceding cases. F D is the cut-line, G H I the section on the cut-line, T T the tangents, and A K L the pitch-board.

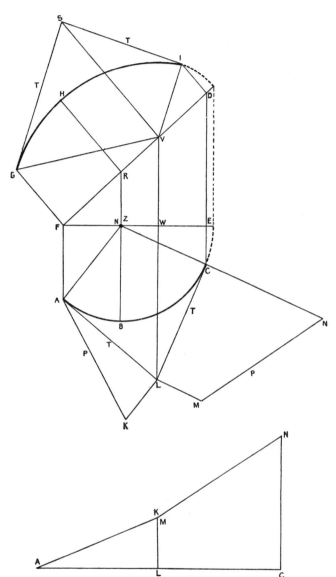

Fig. 957.—Wreath with Plan greater than a Quarter-Circle and Pitches unequal

THE SECTION OF A CYLINDER

If any cylindric body, as A B O (fig. 958), standing on a horizontal plane, is cut by an oblique plane, v o *p*, it is obvious that a third or vertical plane, v P B *p*, may be so applied to the cylinder that it shall not only be at right angles to the ground plane, but also to the plane of section. On such a vertical plane the oblique plane would be projected as a right line, as v *p*. It is evident, then, that if any figure whatever be described on the ground plane *h* P, and it be required to describe on the oblique plane v o *p* such a figure that its various parts in every point shall be immediately over the figure on *h* P, nothing more is necessary than to draw lines through the various parts of the figure on *h* P, perpendicular from P B; continue those lines perpendicularly upon the vertical plane P v *p*, and return them on the oblique plane; and then measure on those lines from the line v *p*, the same each to each on the plane v o *p*, as the corresponding lines on the ground plane; thus, the line v 6 will be made equal to P D, the line 5 equal to C, and so of any other line. Those lines are called ordinate lines, and the method is called tracing by ordinates. It is thus particularly described, because unless the process is perfectly understood by the student, he cannot know how to produce the section of a cylinder, or the face-moulds for handrails, geometrically.

To produce the section of a cylinder through any three points on its convex surface (fig. 959). First draw the plan of the cylinder, or part of the cylinder, as A B C. Let A be the lowest point in the section, B the seat of the intermediate height and C the seat of the greatest height. The height on A is nothing, and is therefore a mere point on the plan; the height on the point B is equal to *b h*, and the height on C is equal to C *p*. These heights are sometimes called the *resting-points*. Draw a right line from A, the seat of the lowest point of the section, to C, the point on the plan agreeing to the highest point of the section; draw C *p* perpendicular to C A, and make it equal to the greatest height of the section; join A *p*. Take the intermediate height and apply it to the triangle as a perpendicular on A C; in other words, make *h b* parallel with C *p*, and equal in length to the intermediate height; then draw the line from *b* to B, the seat of the middle height, and it will be the leading ordinate; then at right angles with B *b*, and touching the convex line of the plan of the cylinder, draw *a* B D—this line is the trace of the vertical plane. Draw C P at right angles to *a* B, and passing through the point C on the plan, and make D P equal to C *p*; join P *a*; continue the line *b* B until it intersect the line *a* P at 2. This completes the representation of the vertical plane P *a* D. Draw the ordinates *c*, *d*, and *e* parallel to D P; square out from the line *a* P the corresponding ordinates 1 2 3 4 5 6, and make them respectively equal to the corresponding ordinates on the plan; thus 6 P is equal to D C, 5 is equal to *e*, 4 to *d*, 3 to *c*, 2 to B, and 1 *a* to *a* A, and the mould for the oblique plane will be completed by tracing a

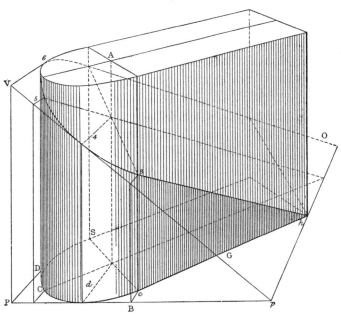

Fig. 958.—Section of a Cylinder by an Oblique Plane

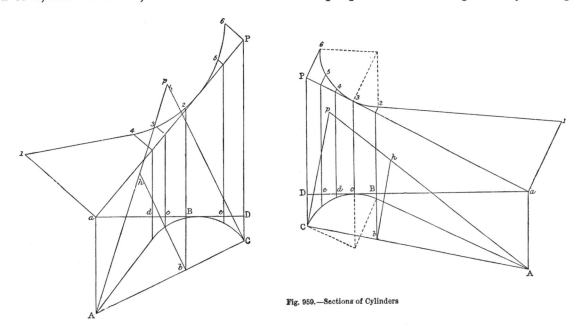

Fig. 959.—Sections of Cylinders

line through the points 1 2 3 4 5 6. The angle *a* P D is what is usually called the pitch of the plank, the use of which will be explained hereafter.

The examples in fig. 960 do not differ in principle from those in fig. 959, but centre lines of the plan of the rail are substituted for the lines A B C. Draw the line A C, connecting the seats of the highest and lowest points; make c *p* equal to the greatest height, and at right angles with A C; make *b h* equal to the intermediate height, and draw the line *b* B, the leading ordinate, as in the preceding figures; square from it for the base of the section, and make all the ordinates on the plan parallel with the leading ordinate *b* B.   Make D P equal to c *p*, the height of the section; draw P *a*, and continue the ordinates to meet it; square them out from *a* P, and make each ordinate on the section equal to its relative ordinate on the plan; draw the curves through the various points 1 2 3, &c., and the moulds will be completed.   In drawing the first triangle, A c *p* the line c *p* may be made equal to the *whole*

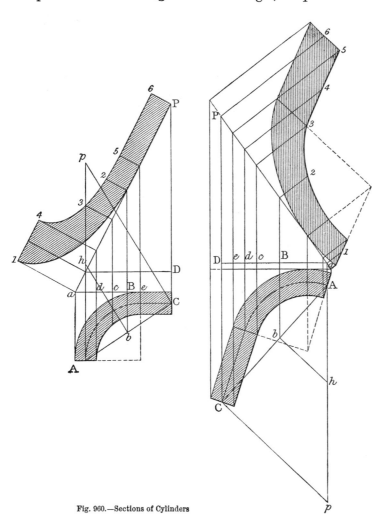

Fig. 960.—Sections of Cylinders

height, or to any fraction of the height, provided the intermediate height be drawn in the same manner; for it is evident that if the perpendicular c *p* be lengthened or shortened, the perpendicular *b h* will be lengthened or shortened in the same proportion; and it will sometimes be found more convenient to use a part than the whole of the height, as will be seen in constructing the moulds, Plate LXXIV.

Tangent and Bevel (fig. 961). —Let the quadrant A B C indicate the ground-plan of the centre line of the wreath, and let I be the centre from which the quadrant is drawn.   Divide A C into two equal parts at B, and join B I.   Through I, at right angles to B I, draw O D, which is called the seat, and from the points A and C draw A O and C D parallel to B I, or at right angles to O D.   Extend C D to E, making D E equal to the given height or rise.   Join E O by the line E K O, cutting B I produced at K, and from O, K, and E erect the perpendiculars O F, K G, and E H, making O F = O A, K G = I B, and E H = D C.   The points F, G, and H will lie in the elliptic curve required.   The tangents are the lines A R and R C, drawn at right angles to A I and C I on the ground-plan.   To find the tangents for the elliptic curve: from the point R, where the two tangents meet, draw the line R B I K till it touches the cutting-line E K O at K, and from this point and at right angles to E K O draw K L equal to I R.   Join L F and L H to obtain the lines of tangents for the elliptic curve.

To find the bevel: from the point L, on the tangent line L H, draw L M parallel to R I on ground-plan, and L P parallel to O E, and on L P take any point N, and from this point, with radius N 8, describe the arc 8 P; from N draw N M at right angles to L P.   N P M will form the bevel.

The bevel can also be found on the ground-plan.   From R, with radius R 6, describe the arc 6 X and join X A.   A X R will form the bevel required.

The ordinate in this and similar cases is always the diagonal of a square, as R I, and the seat must be drawn at right angles to it, as O D. The ordinate is the line from which the angles of the tangents for any portion of a cylinder are found, and furnishes the only reliable method of finding the bevels for joints.

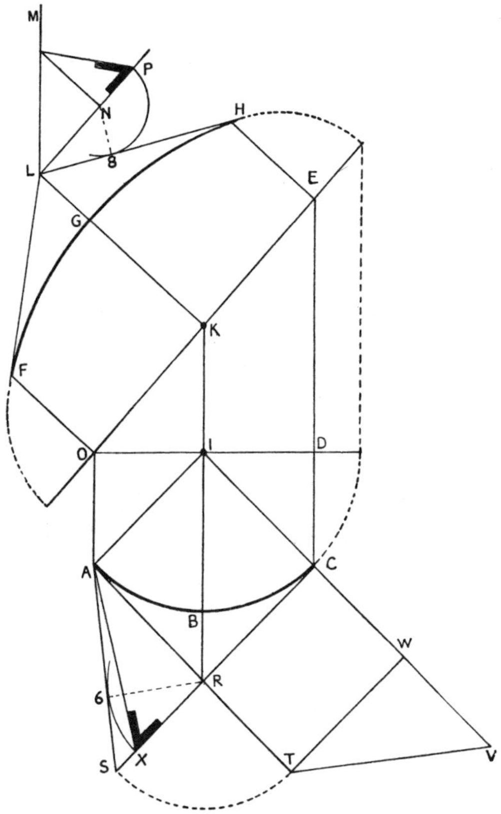

The bevel can also be obtained as shown in fig. 962. From D on the elliptic curve draw D F parallel to the height-line E B, and C D parallel to the cut-line A B, and from any point G on C D, with radius G H, describe the arc C H, and from G, at right angles to C D, draw G F. Join C F and the angle F C D will form the bevel.

Fig. 963 shows the application of bevels.

In Plate LXXIV, fig. 1 shows the face mould, and fig. 2 the falling mould of a rail suited to the stairs, fig. 1, Plate LXXI. For the falling mould describe the quadrant B 3 (fig. 2) to the radius of the concave side of the rail on the plan, and make D B equal to its development; then set out the lines

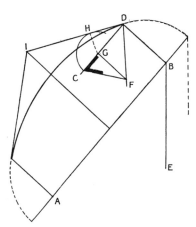

Fig. 962.—Alternative Method of finding Bevel

Fig. 961.—Method of finding Tangents and Bevel

of steps and risers in the order they occur in the stairs, placing all the risers at their proper situation as to the springing and centre lines; make 1 equal to the last flier, 2 equal to the

first winder, 3, 4, 5, and 6 equal to the succeeding winders, taken on the concave curve of the rail; draw the bottom lines of the falling mould, making them touch the angles of the steps except where the curved part necessarily leaves them; draw a line for the centre line of the falling mould at a distance from the bottom equal to half the depth of the rail, also a line at the distance answering to the top of the rail, and draw lines at right angles through the thickness of the rail for the butt-joint, as at P and A; draw a line through the centre of the lower butt-joint parallel to D B, meeting P B in C; make the line *b h* perpendicular to *c b*, at or near the centre of the length of the falling mould. We shall then have P C for the greatest height, and *h b* for the intermediate height of the section, the lowest point of the section being the point A in the plan; the seats of

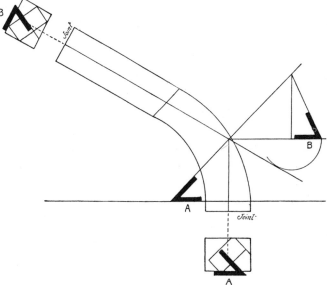

Fig. 963.—Application of Bevels

those points on the plan must always be in the centre line of the rail. To produce the face mould (fig. 1), draw A C, make c p perpendicular thereto, and equal to the greatest height, or to some fraction of the same—in this case it is one-third; then draw the hypotenuse p h A, and take the intermediate height, or its corresponding fraction one-third, and apply it to form the perpendicular b h. From b to the seat of the middle height on the plan, draw the leading ordinate b B, and square the base of the vertical plane as a tangent to the plan mould; draw all the ordinates on the plan parallel to the leading ordinate, and through as many points as may be needed for the tracing; make P f equal to the greatest height, and draw the hypotenuse P a, from which square out all the ordinates, making them respectively equal to the corresponding ones on the plan; carry one ordinate through the centre of the plan, and take off the distance of that point, applying it as at n. Draw the dotted line n 4, and make the butt-joint at 6 by squaring from n 4 through the centre of the bevel-joint. Make the butt-joint at the straight part by simply squaring it from the side of the mould through the centre of the bevel-joint; then trace through the points 1 2 3 4, &c., and the mould will be complete.

Figs. 3 and 4 of this plate are drawn on the same principle. They are introduced as a specimen of a wreath of a small well-hole, with a very sharp ascent, the radius of the inner curve being only 3 inches with three winders in the quarter-space. The risers are here supposed to be drawn to the centre, the riser between the last flier and the first winder is consequently identical with the springing line; the same line is also here made the line of the middle height. The falling mould (fig. 4) is constructed, as before described, with the undersides touching the angles of the steps, except only where made conformable to a fair curve; the height of the section is found, as in the former case, by drawing a horizontal line through the joint line at A, and taking the height from this line to P for the greatest height, both it and the intermediate height being taken to the centre line of the falling mould. A line is drawn in fig. 3, through two of the seat points, namely, A and C; one-third of the greatest height is used as a perpendicular, and the same fraction is used for the middle height, b h; the leading ordinate is drawn through the seat of the middle height, that is, through the centre of the springing line; the base of the vertical plane is squared from the leading ordinate, and the entire height of the section set up at P 1; having drawn P a, and continued and squared out the ordinates, the mould is pricked off by making each ordinate 1 2 3 4, &c., equal to its respective ordinate on the plan. The butt-joint is drawn by squaring it from the line, n g, through the centre of the bevel-joint.

In this case the sharp pitch of the mould produces it a great width at each end; if this were to be cut out of the plank to its proper bevel, C P a, it would take at least *twice* the amount of material that would be needed by the means we shall now point out. Let the centre line be pricked out on the mould, parallel with which draw the dotted line, shown on the same. Now if the mould be laid on the plank in this form it will appear as at fig. 5; this may be cut quite square out of the plank, and will be sufficient to produce the rail in the most perfect shape; C D shows the edge of the plank, the oblique line C D being the proper bevel just mentioned, which is to be drawn on the edge of the plank; A B is drawn on the mould when in its position in fig. 3, as a parallel to P a, and is called the backing line; this line should be drawn on the plank on both sides, and perfectly opposite on each. When the piece has been cut out square, as shown at fig. 5, the point e of the mould should be slid to the point C, where the mould is a second time to be marked on the material, keeping the line A B on the mould to agree with the line A B on the plank; then let the mould be applied to the other side of the plank, by bringing the point e on the mould to coincide with the point D on the plank, and the line A B on the mould to coincide with the line A B on the piece; mark the piece again in this position of the mould; this is what is called backing the mould, and the piece is now properly lined for wreathing. This is done by placing the piece in the vice with the concave edge upwards, and taking off the superfluous

PLATE LXXIV

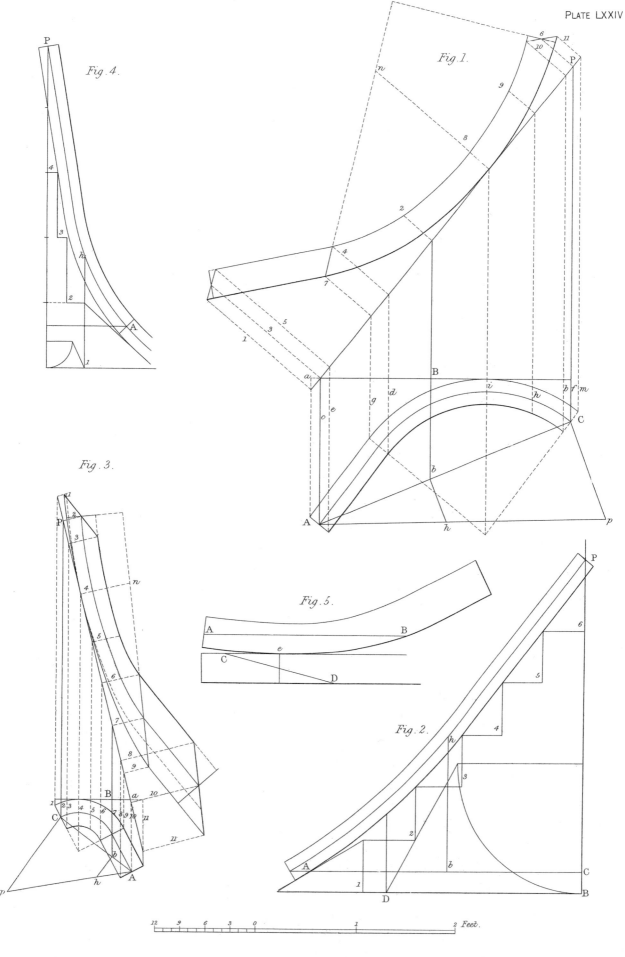

Fig. 4.

Fig. 1.

Fig. 3.

Fig. 5.

Fig. 2.

12 9 6 3 0   1   2 Feet.

HAND RAILING

wood down to the lines just described on the surface of the plank. It will, however, be found requisite sometimes to place the mould on the piece, and fix both in the vice together, in order to supply that portion of the line which will be deficient by reason of cutting square through the plank, instead of the old method of bevelling. When the concave cylindric surface is thus produced, the falling mould may be applied. This is done by making the bevel-joint line of the falling mould to correspond with the bevel-joint line of the piece, while the butt-joint lines of the falling mould also coincide with the butt-joints of the piece; the butt-joints of the falling mould thus applied will now show the position of the joint one way, whilst those of the face mould will show it the other, thus rendering the joint complete; mark on the piece on each side of the falling mould for the under side and top side of the rail; square from the concave surface, both for the top and bottom of the rail, and take off the superfluous wood, using a pair of callipers to gauge off the back side of the piece. What has here been stated will hold good as a general rule; but if the face mould is not much wider than the rail itself, it would be absurd to be at any undue trouble to save material. It will, however, generally be best to cut the piece out square from the plank, and bevel it after in the manner described.

Plate LXXV.—Fig 1 is the falling mould, and fig. 2 the face mould of a wreath suitable for the stairs shown in Plate LXXI, fig. 2.[1] Fig. 1 shows the stretch-out (B D) of A B, the internal curve of the plan. D L is the width of the last flier, 2 3 and 4 are widths of winders. 5 is the half-width of the landing; the line L D, fig. 1, is equal to Ag, fig. 2, or the length of the straight part on the plan; the lines $c\,d\,e\,f$ and P, fig. 1, are all at equal distance from each other, and represented at fig. 2 by the portions of radii $g\,k\,l$, &c., drawn across the rail. The position of the oblique plane is found here (fig. 2) as in Plate LXXIV, c p being a third of the greater height, and $b\,h$ a third of the intermediate height; and as B is the seat of that height, b B becomes the leading ordinate, and a B D the base of the vertical plane; P a is the pitch of the plank; the lines $t\,r$ and $u\,s$ show the upper and lower surfaces of the plank; E F is drawn parallel with a P at any convenient distance; p and q are drawn through each end of the joint line, and continued to the height from the line B a, equal to the distance from E to the section of the falling mould at P, fig. 1. The section of the square rail is thus shown by the small parallelogram at P; in like manner the section of the rail is shown at f from the section of falling mould at f, fig. 1; the parallelograms e, d, c, and a are produced in the same manner from e, d, c, and a in fig. 1. Now draw lines through the angles of each parallelogram, and square with the line E F; the mould is then produced by making the ordinates 18 and 19 (measured from the line E F) equal to q on the plan, the one answering for the top, and the other for the bottom, of the representation of the piece; 20 and 21 are both equal to p on the plan; 14 and 15 are equal to o on the plan, 16 and 17 to n, 10 and 11 to m, 12 and 13 to l, and the other points are traced in a similar way, and parallelograms are then drawn through the points, as seen in the plate; each of these parallelograms will represent a section of the solid square rail as it would appear on the plane of the plank drawn by orthographic projection; if lines be drawn through these angles, they will represent the square rail; such a mould may be laid on the plank, and the piece cut square out; the piece is then set out on the edge, as shown in the elevation, by the vertical sections of the square rail; the distances of the angles may be measured and set off, and each angle found with great precision, first finding the outside angle of the piece, and then gauging the other angles therefrom.

Fig. 3 of this plate shows the manner of setting out a wreath for such a situation as that exhibited by the landing stairs, fig. 1, Plate LXIX. A C is the length of the straight part at the upper end of the piece, C D the length of the circular, and D B the length of the straight part at the lower end of the piece. Make L the landing, equal to the develop-

---

[1] This plate exhibits the method of cutting the wreath out square, as first taught by Nicholson, but is not contained in his *Carpenter's Guide.*

ment of C D, and the half-steps *r* and *g h*, equal respectively to A C and D B; bisect C D and draw E F; make the perpendicular at *g* equal to half a riser, also the same at G; make the perpendicular at F equal to half a riser from L the landing line; set off the half-width of the falling mould above *h*, and draw the bottom line of the falling mould by making the hypotenuse lines at *r* and *h*; connect these by a fair curve passing through the proper height at F; draw also the centre line and top of the falling mould. It will be seen that if the usual method of finding the position of the oblique plane were here applied, it would necessarily produce the line *g* as the leading ordinate, for the height F is half the height *k* G, and the base *k i* is bisected by the line F; consequently the hypotenuse should in like manner be bisected by placing the intermediate height. This fact is mentioned to show that there are many cases occurring where a moment's reflection will serve to convince the practical man what the position of the plank should be, without drawing one line. Therefore for the face mould (see fig. 4) bisect the quadrant in *g*, and draw the ordinate *g*, from which square the ordinates from D a, and also from the hypotenuse, and make the ordinates 1 2 3 4, &c., equal to the corresponding ordinates *a b c d*, &c.; and draw the face mould through the respective points; to produce the butt-joint, square from the side of the rail through the centre of the bevel-joint.

The application of the falling mould is shown in fig. 5; the line F of the falling mould (fig. 3) is placed in the position *g*, answering to *g* on the plan, and in the centre of the thickness of the plank; s and s show the springing lines, A and B the bevel-joints; a butt-joint is shown at the lower end of the piece: its application will be easily comprehended, and will generally serve for the performance of this work. No example of a perfectly straight falling mould has been given, as it would be superfluous; it will be easily seen, from what has been said, that the leading ordinate in such cases must always fall in the same manner as in the last instance.

Plate LXXVI exhibits the manner of producing the falling moulds and face moulds for scrolls. In fig. 1, No. 1 is the face mould, and No. 2 the falling mould, for a small scroll. In tracing moulds of this description there is no need of any process to find the position of the plank; no better position can be found than that in which a plank would be if laid flat on the nosings of the stairs, and the pitch-board gives this angle of inclination. Take the pitch-board, and lay the step side of it against the side of the straight part of the plan mould A B, and by means of the upper edge of the pitch-board mark off the line *c d*; draw any number of ordinates on the plan mould square with the straight rail, continue them to *c d*, square them out, and prick off the mould by making the ordinates *f g h i k l*, respectively, equal to the ordinates 1 2 3 4 5 on the plan mould, and draw the face mould through the points. This mould may be drawn without using more ordinates than are needed to find the joint, and to show the width of the straight rail. The mould itself is merely a quarter of an ellipse, both for the inner and outer curves, and its transverse diameter is equal to the diameter of that circle from which it is generated on the plan; therefore if the ordinate *f* be continued till equal to the length of radius, it will represent so much of the transverse diameter, and a line drawn through its extremity, parallel to *c d*, will represent the conjugate diameter of the ellipse, and the mould may be produced by the trammel, or by any of the means explained in Section V. The shaded part *a b* shows the piece wrought and in position.

The falling mould, No. 2, is produced by making the line *e*, 1 2 3, &c., equal to the line *e*, 1 2 3, &c., in No. 1, on the convex side of the rail. From the top of the ordinate line 1, draw the line *b* to the pitch of the rail, and connect this line to the line 9 *e*, by a fair curve; this forms the bottom line of the falling mould; the top line is drawn parallel to it at a distance equal to the depth of the rail. The ordinates 1 2 3, &c., will now show the height of the rail, in as many points, from the bottom of the scroll. The falling mould, No. 3, is produced by making the line, 1 2 3, &c., equal to the internal curve of the scroll, and the ordinates 1 2 3, &c., on No. 3, equal to the ordinates 1 2 3, &c., on No. 2; the piece is

PLATE LXXV

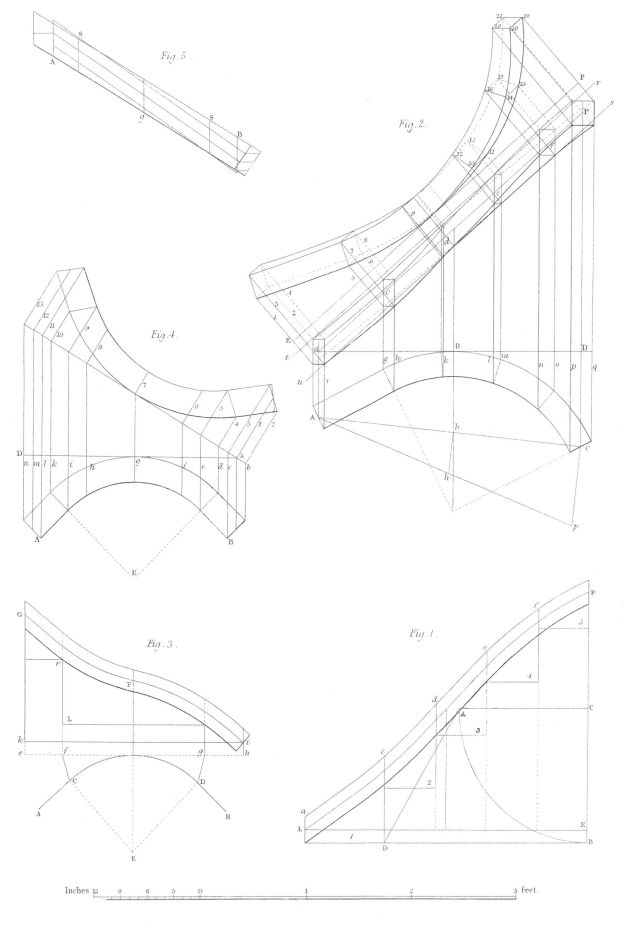

Fig. 5.

Fig. 2.

Fig. 4.

Fig. 3.

Fig. 1.

Inches 12   9   6   3   0   1   2   3 Feet.

HAND RAILING

jointed at A on the plan (No. 1) to the level portion of the scroll, the line 5 on the falling mould (No. 3) showing the same as a perpendicular joint, differing little from a butt-joint, which might, of course, be used if preferred.

Fig. 2 of this plate exhibits the side view of two pieces of handrail of similar character to the scroll pieces just described, but applied to a landing, m being the landing, o the riser, and n the step below; whilst l shows the riser, and k the step above. Such a landing may be seen in plan at c, fig. 1, Plate LXXI, being the top of the first flight of stairs. The risers in this case do not pass through the centre of the well-hole; they are so arranged that the centre B of the rail on the return shall be precisely half a step from the line of risers, l o. By this arrangement the piece of rail in this part is of the simple kind just mentioned, less indent of the well-hole into the landing is made, and the rail itself has a better appearance than when a greater amount of it is thrown on the level at the landing. The pitch-board is applied with its step side against the side of the plan mould, as at A, and the pitch-line produces the line A a. Draw all the ordinates, 1, 2, 3, &c., parallel to the riser line of the pitch-board, and return them on the plane of the mould or plank at right angles to A a; make the ordinates a, b, c, &c., equal to the ordinates 1, 2, 3, &c., on the plan, and draw the mould. This mould, as also the preceding one for the scroll, must be bevelled by the pitch-board. Lay, therefore, the hypotenuse of the pitch-board to coincide with the surface of the plank, and the riser line of the board will give the bevel on the edge of the plank for backing the mould; this will be better comprehended by the position the piece will have when placed in the work, as shown by C D and E F.

In fig. 3 is shown another and somewhat more expeditious method of working. Let B c be the plan mould, with its centre line as shown, and h e d the pitch; square out the line d f and make it equal to e c; then square out from the ordinate h, making it also equal to e c. The semiconjugate and semitransverse diameters of the elliptical mould will thereby be obtained, and it may be drawn by the trammel, or by any of the methods already mentioned. It is possible, by thus working to the centre line only, to make the rail without cutting it out one-eighth of an inch wider in any place than its *exact* width.

Fig. 4 shows the same piece cut out from the square plank; the end is then, by the use of the pitch-board, to have the line a drawn through the centre of its thickness; which enables us to draw the centre line of the mould f (fig. 3) on the piece, as shown by the curve line at a. By using a pair of callipers the vertical sides of the rail may be readily produced, and the bottom and top squared from them.

Fig. 5 shows, at No. 1, the scroll adapted for such a stair as the elliptical stair, Plate LXXII, or wherever a scroll comes immediately in connection with winders. First decide at what point on the plan mould the scroll shall come to its level position; and as the plank is usually about ½ inch more in thickness than the rail is in depth, it will be possible to obtain that extent of rising in the first part or level portion of the scroll; this is supposed to be at the point g on the plan mould, which is therefore made the place of the first joint. The point c is that point of the rail where the third riser occurs, and may with propriety be made the place of the second joint. Take the stretch-out of the exterior curve, d to g, and make the line c g, in No. 2, equal thereto, and set out the bottom line A B of the falling mould 2 inches below c g. On A B set off the height of the rail at c equal to two risers; draw the line l to the inclination of the rail, and the intermediate portion of the falling mould, as a fair curve, connecting the straight lines; make the centre and top lines of the falling mould parallel to the bottom line, to suit the depth of the rail. This completes the falling mould. For the face mould, in No. 1, draw through the centres of the joint lines the line c g; make c d perpendicular thereto and equal to c d in No. 2, and draw d g. Take the distance c e from No. 2, and set it out from a to b, No. 1, and make the point b in the centre of the width of the rail; this will be the seat of the intermediate height, and c and g the seats of the highest and lowest heights. Take the length of e f, No. 2, and apply it at e f,

No. 1, parallel to *d c*; draw the line *e b* for the leading ordinate and square from it, as a tangent to the curve of the scroll; draw *b t*, the base line for the wreath, and draw *t s* and *g n* perpendicular to *b t*, then draw the hypotenuse, and continue the ordinates *a i k l m*, &c., to meet it. From the points of intersection draw the ordinates 1 2 3 4 5 6 7, &c., making them respectively equal to the ordinates *a h i k b l m*, &c.; and through the points thus obtained prick off the mould.

SECTIONS OF HANDRAILS.—In fig. 964 four sections of handrails are given. To describe No. 1, divide the width 6 6 in twelve parts, bisect it by the line A B, at right angles to 6 6;

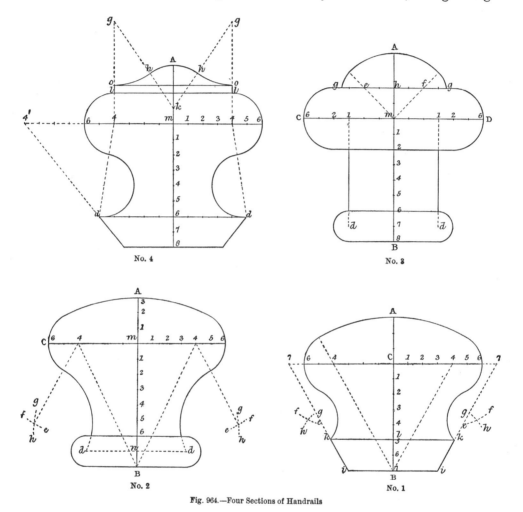

Fig. 964.—Four Sections of Handrails

make C B equal to seven, A C equal to three such parts, and B *i* also equal to three parts; set off one part on the horizontal line from 6 to 7, draw the lines 7 *i* on each side of the figure; set the compasses in 4 4, extend them to 6 6, and describe the arcs at 6 6 to form the sides of the figure; also set the compasses in B, extending them to A, and describe the arc at A to form the top; make *l* B equal to two parts, and draw the line *k l k*; take four parts in the compasses, and from the points 4 4 on the horizontal line describe the arcs *e f*, then with two parts in the compasses, one foot being placed in *k*, draw the intersecting arcs *g h*; from these intersections as centres, describe the remaining portions of the curves, and by joining *k i*, *k i*, complete the figure.

No. 2 is another similar section of handrail. The width 6 6 is divided into twelve equal parts as before; the point 4 is the centre for the side of the figure, which is described with a radius of two parts; A *m* is made equal to three parts, and B *m* to eight parts, and *m n* equal to seven parts; then will A B be the radius, and B the centre for the top of the rail.

PLATE LXXVI

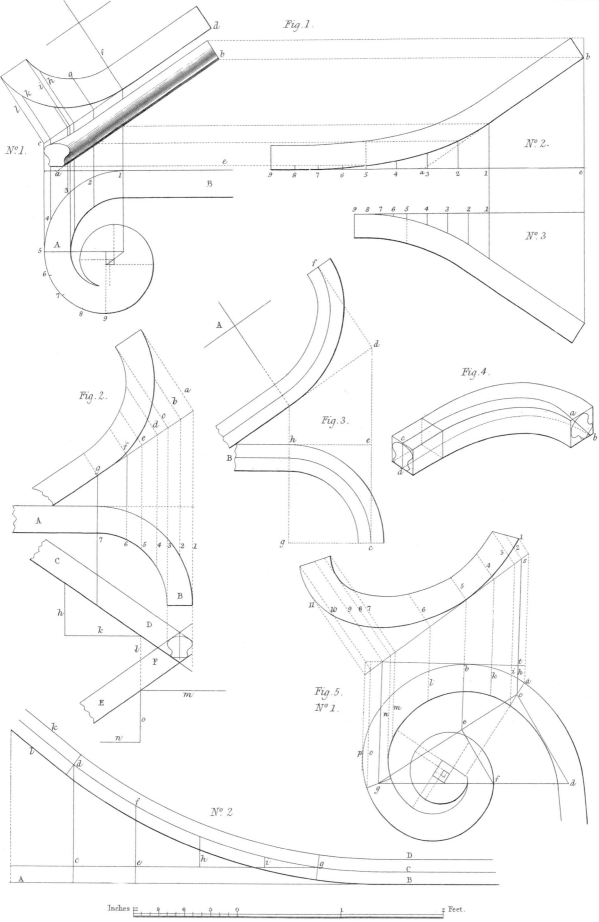

HAND RAILING

Take seven parts in the compasses, and from the centre 6 in the vertical line A B describe the arcs *g h, g h*; take six parts in the compasses, and from the centre 4 describe the arcs *e f, e f*; draw the line *d d* through the point *n*; from the intersections at *e f g h*, as a centre, with the radius of four parts, and from 4, as a centre, with the radius of two parts, describe the curve of contrary flexure forming the side of the rail; then from *d*, with the radius of one part, describe the arc at *d*, forming the astragal for the bottom of the rail.

In No. 3 divide the width C D into twelve equal parts; make 6 B and *m h*, respectively, equal to two parts, *m* 1 equal to three parts; and *e h* and *h f*, respectively, equal to two parts, then in *f* and *e* set one foot of the compasses, and with a radius equal to one and a half parts, describe the arcs *g g*; from the point *m* describe the arc at A meeting the arcs *g g*, to form the top reed of the figure; from 2, with a radius equal to two parts, describe the side reeds C and D; draw 1 *d* parallel to A B; and with a radius of one part from the points *d d* describe the reed *d* for the bottom of the rail.

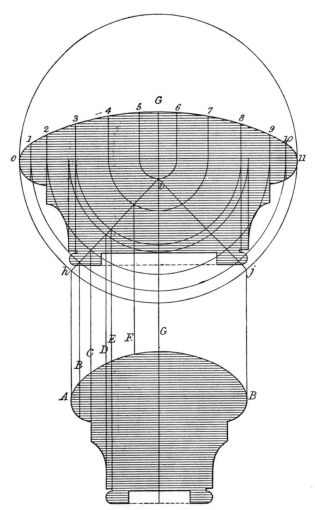

To describe No. 4 let the width 6 6 be divided into 12 parts; and set off eight similar parts from *m* to 8; through 6 in the vertical line draw *d d*, making 6 *d* equal to 5 parts, and draw the dotted lines *d* 4; also the lines 4 *g*. On these lines make *l* 4 equal to two parts, *l o* equal to half a part, and *o g* equal to four parts; also make *m k* equal to one part, and draw the lines *g k*; from *g* describe the arcs *h o*, and from *k* describe the arc at A for the top of the rail. At 4 and 4, with the radius of two parts, describe the arcs at 6 for the sides of the rail; then from *d* set off the distance of two parts on the line *d* 4, and from this point as a centre, with a radius of two parts, describe the curves of contrary flexure terminating in *d d*, which will complete the curved parts of the figure. Continue the line 6 6 the distance of four parts on each side to the points 4': and from these points, through the points *d d*, draw the lines for the chamfers at the bottom of the rail.

Fig. 965.—Section of Mitre-Cap produced from Section of Handrail

Modern architects do not, as a rule, adopt such laborious methods for the delineation of handrails. The principal lines are set out by the T-square and set-square, and the mouldings are then drawn by hand.

To form the Section of the Mitre-Cap.—Fig. 965 exhibits the method of producing the section of the mitre-cap at the top of a newel from the section of the handrail.

Let A B C D, &c., be the section of the handrail. Draw the line G G in the centre of the section, and draw across it, at right angles, the line A B; describe a circle 0, 11, *j*, *h*, having its centre on the line G G, and its diameter equal to the size of the cap. From the outsides of the rail A B, draw lines A *h*, B *j*, parallel to the line G G, and meeting the circle of the cap at *h j*. From the points of intersection *h j*, draw lines meeting on the line G G at a point *i*, as far into the mitre-cap as it is proposed to carry the mitre. Then draw lines parallel to

G G, through as many points in the rail as may be required, as B C D E F, continuing them till they meet the mitre lines $hi, ji,$; set one foot of the compasses in the centre of the circle 0 11 jh, and extending the other to each of the points in succession, describe circular arcs meeting the diameter 0 11.   From the points of meeting draw the ordinates 1 2 3 4 5, &c., making them respectively equal to the corresponding ordinates B C D E F, &c., and draw the figure through those points.

To draw the Swan-Neck at the Top of a Rail, as in fig. 931, No. 1.—Continue the bottom line of the rail upwards till it intersects the line of the back of the last baluster; draw a horizontal line through the top of the newel, measure from this line down the back of the baluster to the intersection, and set off the same distance downwards on the under side of the rail, from which square

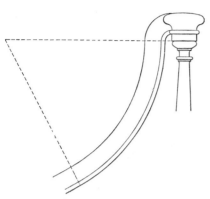

Fig. 966.—Swan-neck and Mitre-Cap

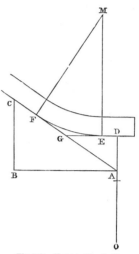

Fig. 967.—Knee in Handrail

out a line to intersect the horizontal line above; this will give the centre point of the curve. A slight variation from this will be seen in fig. 966, the rail being there brought nearer to the newel.   This variation will be easily understood, and needs no description.

To form the Knee at the Bottom Newel.—Draw out the width of one step, as at A B (fig. 967), and the risers B C and O A connected with it above and below, and join A C; continue the line of the first riser O A upwards to the height of half a riser at D; and through D draw a horizontal line meeting the hypotenuse A G in G.   From D set off towards G, half the width of the mitre-cap D E, make G F equal to G E; draw F M square from the under side of the rail, and make E M perpendicular to D G, and the point M will be the centre of the curve.

Scrolls.—In fig. 968 is shown a very simple manner of describing a scroll.   Take the width of the rail in the dividers, and repeat it three times on the line 1 2 3 in No. 1, which gives the first or greatest radius for the quadrant A.   Refer now to No. 2, where the scheme of

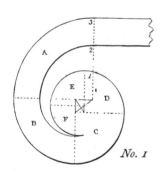

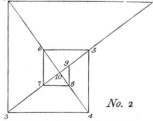

Fig. 968.—Simple Scroll for Handrail

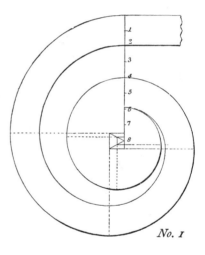

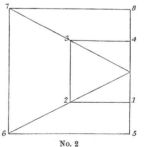

Fig. 969.—Second Method of describing a Scroll

centres is drawn out at full size.   Draw 1 2 at right angles to the first line, and make it equal to two-thirds the width of the rail.   Draw 2 3 at right angles to 1 2; make it equal to three-fourths of 1 2, and join 3 1; through 2, and at right angles to 3 1, draw the line 2 4; then draw the line 3 4 at right angles to 3 2, the line 4 5 at right angles to 3 4, or parallel to 3 2, and so on with the other lines, always squaring from the one last drawn, and thus the centres are obtained, from which the quadrants B, C, D, E, F in No. 1 are drawn.

In fig. 969 the rail is $2\frac{3}{4}$ inches in width. The square for the centres is made half of that width, or $1\frac{3}{8}$ inch, and the first radius $7\frac{1}{2}$ times the square, and as the side of the square is once lost by the half-revolution, the width of the scroll will be equal to 14 times the side of the square, or $19\frac{1}{4}$ inches; the construction of the square will easily be understood by a reference to No. 2, where it is shown full size, the numbers showing the points for the centres in succession, beginning with the least radius, and ending with the greatest.

Fig. 970 is perhaps more simple than the preceding, and is adapted for a large rail, where only a small scroll can be used. The first radius is made equal to 8 inches. This distance is divided into five equal parts, and the square is made equal to one of the parts. The angles of the square are the first four centres, the middle of the side is the fifth, and the centre of the square the sixth centre.

Fig. 971 shows a ready method of producing a converging series in geometrical progression, as such a series is often found useful in setting off the radii of scrolls. The lengths

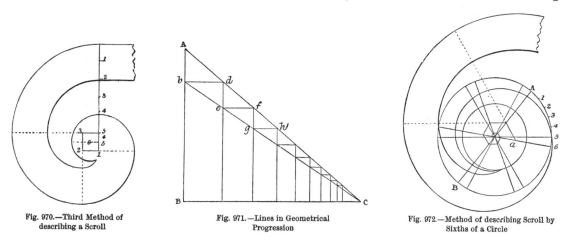

Fig. 970.—Third Method of describing a Scroll

Fig. 971.—Lines in Geometrical Progression

Fig. 972.—Method of describing Scroll by Sixths of a Circle

of any two lines being known, to form a series from the same: take the longest line, as A B, and make it the perpendicular of a right-angled triangle, the base of which B C may be made of any convenient length; let the vertical line d be the length of the second line in the series; join A d and produce the line till it meets the base B C at C; from d draw $d\,b$ perpendicular to A B and join b C, cutting the vertical d in the point e; draw $e\,f$ perpendicular to A B, then draw $f\,g$ perpendicular to B C, and $g\,h$ perpendicular to A B; this process may be continued to any extent, and the lines A B, d, f, h, &c., and also $b\,e$, $e\,g$, &c., and $b\,d$, $e\,f$, $g\,h$, &c., will be series in geometrical progression.

Fig. 972 is a method of producing a scroll by sixths of a circle. Describe a circle as A B, and divide its circumference into six equal parts, and draw the diameters shown by the darker lines on the drawing. Divide one of the divisions of the circle into six equal parts, and set off one of the divisions (equal to 10 degrees) from each diameter; then draw the second series of diameters shown by fainter lines; or the 10 degrees may be set off at once by a protractor. At the distance of 2 inches from the centre draw the first service-line a parallel to the faint diameter and intersecting A B; from the point of intersection draw the next service-line parallel to the next faint diameter, intersecting the next succeeding darker-lined diameter, and so on. The lines so drawn form a converging series, and their lengths are to each other in geometrical progression. In the figure the series is continued from a inwards, through one revolution and a half, a being the centre from which the outermost part of the stroll is struck.

Fig. 973 shows three methods of drawing scrolls by eighths of a circle. As they differ only in the quickness of their convergency a description of one will suffice for all. In No. 1

proceed first to make the double cross by drawing right angles and bisecting the same, as shown on the figure.   The centre of the largest arc of this scroll is situated at a distance of 2 inches from the centre of the scroll to the right, on the line b.   Then set off $2\frac{1}{4}$ inches on the next diameter from the centre to the point a, and join $a\,b$.   The most ready method of producing the converging service-lines is by cutting a small piece of paper to the angle at a, and using this as a bevel to the next diameter, and so on in succession, either converging or diverging; thus the angle of service-line and diameter, taken at a, may be applied at b, at c, and so on in succession, producing each centre by its intersection with the next diameter.   The service-lines $c\,b\,a$ are continued out in the open space of the scroll

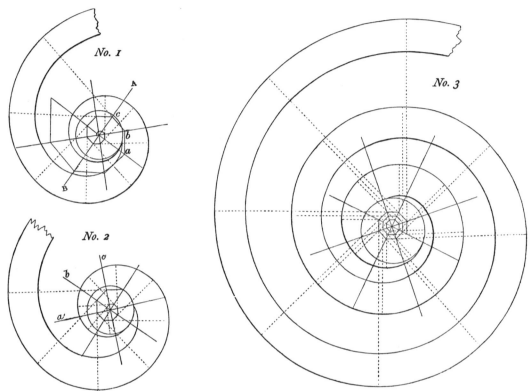

Fig. 973.—Methods of describing Scrolls by Eighths of a Circle.

in this figure, beyond where their use occurs, so that the manner of obtaining one from the other may be the better seen.

Fig. 974 shows a vertical scroll, sometimes used for terminating a handrail when space cannot be afforded for a horizontal scroll.   The method of drawing it is obvious.

Fig. 975 is a scroll step suitable for the rail-scroll in No. 1, fig. 973, and the centres of the various arcs are found as in that case, the same centres being used for the line of balusters and the line of nosings; then, to describe the block and step, take the length of radius of one of the arcs in the rail mould from its centre to the centre of the rail, and from its corresponding centre in the block, which will extend to the centre of the baluster, as from c to e; draw out the section of the baluster e to the intended size; then extend the compasses from the centre of the curve to the inside of the baluster, and describe from each centre in succession, to produce the interior curve of the block.   The width of the block at its neck, that is at g, should always be commensurate with the size of the baluster, as there shown; from this place the outer or convex line of the block is determined, and is struck round from the same centres as before, which are also used for the nosing line, thereby showing the size of the stepboard.   At a is shown what is usually called the tail of the block.   It is secured by a screw to the thick part of the riser.   At i is shown the shoulder of the riser; from this point the riser is reduced to a veneer, which is carried round the convex portion of the block as far as the point *h*, where it is secured by a pair of counter-wedges, there shown in section. On the back part of the step is a line indicating the position of the second riser of the stairs, and the section of the baluster on the second step is shown; from this baluster to the next at *e* should be equal to half the going of one step;

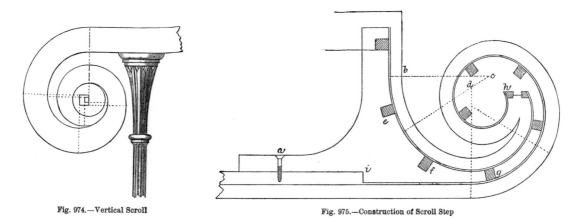

Fig. 974.—Vertical Scroll   Fig. 975.—Construction of Scroll Step

and in spacing the balusters round the scroll, it is desirable that their distances from each other should gradually diminish as they approach nearer to the centre of the scroll, and that the balusters of the inner revolution should be as nearly as possible in the centres between those of the outer revolution; otherwise they will look crowded and irregular.

Section X

Part I.—AIRTIGHT-CASE MAKING

By EDWARD B. BAKER

Part II.—WOOD-TURNING

By R. W. COLE, B.A.

Section X
Part I.—AIRTIGHT-CASE MAKING
By EDWARD B. BAKER

My aim in preparing this small treatise has been to supply the necessary information for enabling a practical joiner or cabinet-maker to become a competent airtight-case maker,

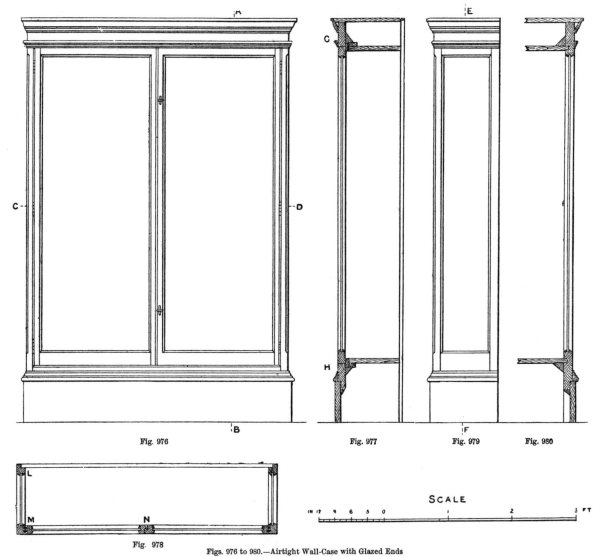

Fig. 976   Fig. 977   Fig. 979   Fig. 980

SCALE

Fig. 978

Figs. 976 to 980.—Airtight Wall-Case with Glazed Ends

Fig. 976, Front elevation; fig. 977, vertical section on line A B; fig. 978, horizontal section on line C D; fig. 979, side elevation; fig. 980, vertical section on line E F

without the tedium of waiting, perhaps for years, until chance brings him into contact with one who has made a speciality of this class of work. I have endeavoured, by means of

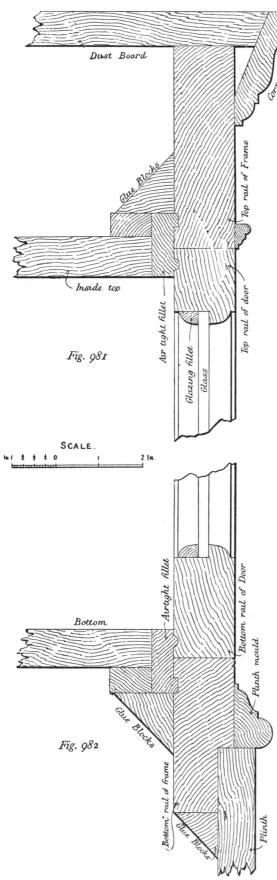

Fig. 981

SCALE.

Fig. 982

Figs. 981 and 982.—Details of Airtight Wall-Case (fig. 977)
Fig. 981, Detail at G; fig. 982, detail at H.

illustrations, to elucidate as clearly as possible the points which are so frequently the cause of failure to those who, while having a good knowledge of wood-working, have not had the advantages of direct practical tuition in the intricacies of airtight-case making.

Before proceeding with the explanations, I would point out that the first and most important rule in joinery is to have the stuff planed up true, and gauged accurately to size.

1. AIRTIGHT WALL-CASE WITH GLASS OR WOOD ENDS

The general drawings of an airtight wall-case with glazed ends are given in figs. 976 to 980, and the details in figs. 981 to 984.

Framework.—Figs. 981 and 982 give the width of the top and bottom rails for the front frame of the case, and, by adding the width of the top and bottom door-rails to each, we determine the width of the rails required for the ends of the case, as shown in fig. 980. The angle-stile must be $\frac{1}{4}$ inch more in thickness than the thickness of the doors, in order to allow of a rebate being formed to receive the glass at the ends of the case (see M, fig. 983).

In setting out the framework (which is mortised and tenoned together in the ordinary way) the face shoulders of the front rails should be $\frac{1}{8}$ inch longer than the back shoulders. An eighth-inch bead—for which the allowance has been made—is worked on the angle-stiles and bottom rail only, the edge of the top rail being left square. The moulding which is planted round the case, as shown in fig. 981, serves to break the joint of the doors. The shoulders on the end rails are square with each other, the rebate being the same depth as the moulding.

Airtight Joints.—To make successfully the airtight joint between the angle-stile of the case and the hanging stile of the door (see fig. 983), three planes are required. The first plane is used on the angle-stile for forming at the same time the two grooves, each $\frac{3}{16}$ inch wide; the second is used for working the two fillets together; and the third for working the two hollows in the door-stiles.

The front part of the frame must now be

fitted together and the joints at the back of the frame cleaned off, to allow the airtight planes to be worked from the back of the frame, that is, from the inside of the case, as the doors would not close accurately if they were worked from the face or outside.

After the front frame has been fitted together as described, it must be taken apart, and the angle-stiles worked with plane No. 1. When this has been done, the fillets must be glued in the grooves, and, when set, rounded over with plane No. 2. The fillets will not require to be taken to the exact width before rounding over, as plane No. 2 works all surplus stuff away.

For the joint between the top and bottom rails of doors and the airtight fillets respectively, two planes are required: the first for sticking the airtight fillet, and the second for working the small hollow on the door-rails to match the fillet.

Continuing with the framework. After rounding the fillets in the angle-stiles, groove the top and bottom rails to receive the tongue on the airtight fillets as shown in figs. 981 and 982, and rebate the bottom rails to rest on the plinth (fig. 982). The top and bottom rails at each end of the case are trenched to receive respectively the ends of the inside top and the inside bottom (see fig. 980). Care must be taken to make these trenches in such a way as to keep the inside top and the inside bottom in the positions shown in figs. 981 and 982. Rebate the back angle-stile of each end frame to receive the back (as in fig. 983), and run a small hollow in the angle of the rebate. Glue and pin the airtight fillet on the front edges of the inside

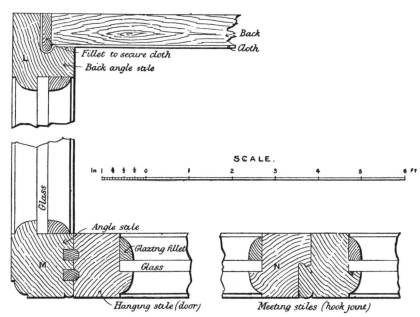

Fig. 983.—Details of Airtight Wall-Case (fig. 978)

top and bottom respectively; also glue the fillet on the back of each in order to strengthen the airtight fillet, and make out the thickness to receive the glue-blocks as shown. An ovolo or other moulding is now worked on the external angles of the two front angle-stiles, as shown in fig. 983, the moulding being stopped on a line with the top and bottom rails respectively of the doors (see fig. 976).

The body of the case must now be put together, care being taken to glue-block the front frame and ends securely to the bottom and top, as well as behind the plinth, which is screwed to the bottom rails from the back.

Match-boards are used for the back, the boards being run to the floor, as shown in fig. 977. Mitre the cornice round the front and ends, screwing it from the back of the top rails; cut the dust-board to fit on the top edges of the rails and bevel against the cornice, having previously rebated it to receive the back of the case. Before the back is fastened, the cloth (fig. 983) should be placed in the rebate of the stile, the fillet placed on top of the cloth and pressed into the hollow, and then fastened to the stile with screws, the cloth thus being securely held between the fillet and the stile. The cloth can now be stretched taut and fixed at the other end in the same way, and the boards fastened in.

Doors.—In planing up the stuff for the doors, the same gauge must be used as that for the frame of the case. When setting out for the doors, take the width and height accurately, and allow $\frac{1}{16}$ inch on the height for fitting in. The width is set out as for ordinary folding doors, viz. allowing half the hook-joint on each door, and $\frac{1}{8}$ inch for jointing and fitting in. The best way to allow for fitting is to have each stile $\frac{1}{16}$ inch greater in width than the finished size required.

The rails abutting against each angle-stile are single-mortised and tenoned together as in ordinary work, but double mortises and tenons must be used at the top and bottom of each meeting stile, as shown in fig. 984. The reason for using the double tenon is, that if a single tenon were used, the ends of the tenon would chip off after the hook-joint had been made.

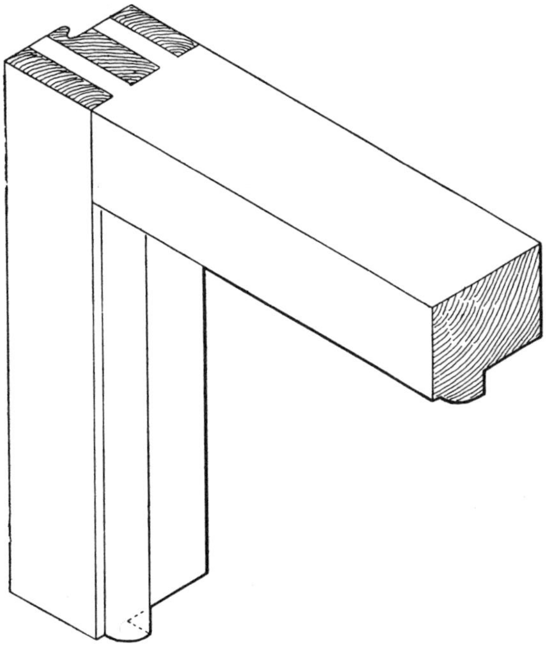

Presuming the doors to be wedged up, level off the joints at the shoulders, when the doors will be ready for jointing together and fitting to the case.

Hook-joint. — The following is the best method of making a well-fitting joint. First rebate the stiles (the rebate being $\frac{1}{8}$ inch less in width than half the thickness of the doors, and $\frac{5}{16}$ inch deep), and next bevel the edges of the doors, bringing the rebate to a depth of $\frac{1}{4}$ inch (see N, fig. 983). The doors must now be worked with a hollow and round on the edge of the rebate to form the hook-joint. For this purpose a hook-joint plane is required. There is an adjustable depth-gauge on the side of the plane, which can be easily set for working different thicknesses of stuff. Before working the doors with the plane, it is advisable to work a piece of stuff of the same thickness as the doors. Cut the piece thus worked into two, and put the joint together. This will test the accuracy of the setting of the plane. If the faces do not come flush with each other, the gauge on the plane must be raised or lowered accordingly.

Fig. 984.—View of Double Tenon of Top Rail (below the haunching)

Having fitted the meeting stiles, place the doors together across the bench, as they can thus be more easily taken to the exact width and height of the frame of the case. After the doors have been fitted in the opening, work with the airtight planes as previously instructed, always remembering to hold the fence of plane No. 3 on the back side of the door while forming the hollows on the hanging stiles. With plane No. 2 the small hollow on the top and bottom rails to match the airtight fillet is worked.

After working the doors as described, clean off the back side, place the doors in position, and clean off the face to the level of the frame. Take the doors out and work the bead on the joint between the doors (fig. 983). This bead is flatter than usual, and has a very small quirk.

The doors are hung to the frame, each by three hinges. The top and bottom hinges are usually kept their own depth from the top and bottom edges of the doors respectively, *e.g.* a $2\frac{1}{2}$-inch hinge will be $2\frac{1}{2}$ inches from the edge. The handles on the meeting stiles are respectively about 9 inches from the upper and lower edges of door.

All glass in the doors must be carefully packed with small slips of wood between the edges of the glass and the frame of the door, in order to keep the frame rigid. The wood-work being so slight, the doors would sag when hung if the glass were not packed tightly, as all the weight of the glass would fall on the bottom rail.

Shelves.—The following is the best method to adopt for fitting the case with shelves, as, when fitted in this way, the shelves can be moved to any required height. To the back of the case screw two pieces of iron, one at each side, extending from the top to the bottom of the case. These must previously have been drilled and tapped their whole length, the space between each hole being $\frac{1}{2}$ inch from centre to centre, and each hole being large enough to receive a $\frac{3}{16}$-inch screw. A malleable-iron bracket about 3 inches long on the back edge—the length of the top edge being the width of the shelf—is now required, having a small piece projecting above the top edge in which is drilled a plain hole, and having a pin near the bottom edge. The pin at the bottom edge is placed in one of the holes in the tapped bar, and a $\frac{3}{16}$-inch screw is passed through the hole at the top edge and screwed into the bar, thus securing the bracket firmly. Care must be taken to have the distance between the centre of the pin on the bracket and the centre of the plain hole equal to the distance between the centres of any two holes in the bar.

Fig. 985 shows a horizontal section through a showcase having solid ends.

Fig. 986 shows a horizontal section through the centre hanging stile in the front frame of a wide showcase, when two pairs of doors are required. It is worked in the same manner as previously described for hanging stiles.

Fig. 987 shows a section of a cross-bar in doors. This is only required where sheet-glass is used.

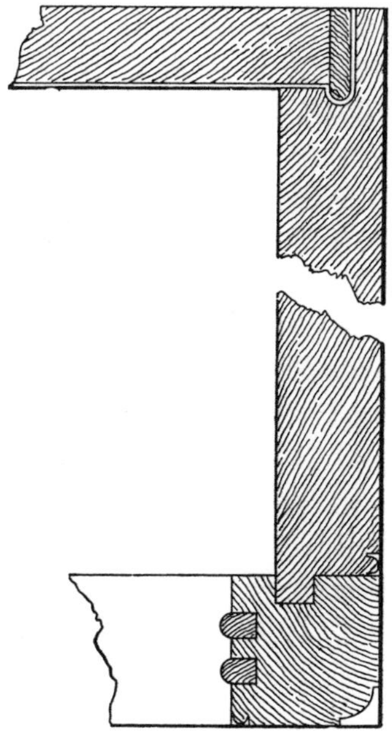

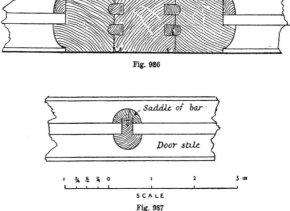

Fig. 985

Fig. 986

Fig. 987

Figs. 985 to 987

Fig. 985, Detail of solid end to wall-case; fig. 986, detail of central hanging stile for folding doors; fig. 987, detail of cross-bar in doors

Each end of the bar is sunk into the moulding of the door-stiles. The saddle is cut between the rebates, and secured to the bar.

Plinths separate from the Case.—If the showcase is over 6 feet 6 inches in height, or the plinth is of a greater depth than 12 inches, it is advisable to make the plinth separate from the case. Instead of the bottom rail being rebated behind the plinth, as shown in fig. 982, a frame must be made out of $1\frac{1}{2}$-inch by 3-inch stuff dovetailed together at the angles; and two or three bearers should be mortised and tenoned between the front and back rails (as the length of the case may require). At each angle, and under each end of the bearers, a leg is stump-tenoned into the under side of the rails to support the case. When this is done, the plinth should be mitred round the frame. It should be screwed from the back, and glue-blocks used in all the angles.

2. AIRTIGHT COUNTER-CASE

An isometrical projection of a counter-case is shown in fig. 988. The top, sides, and front are of plate-glass. Mirrors are placed on the inside of the doors at the back of the case. The divisions on the bottom show the position of the trays.

Before commencing work, it is absolutely necessary to draw figs. 989 to 991 full size, to enable the taking off, and working to an exact size, of the various parts required, to be done.

Bottom of Case.—Commence with the frame, which should be made out of well-seasoned pine. The width of the bottom frame will be the extreme width of the case less the thick-

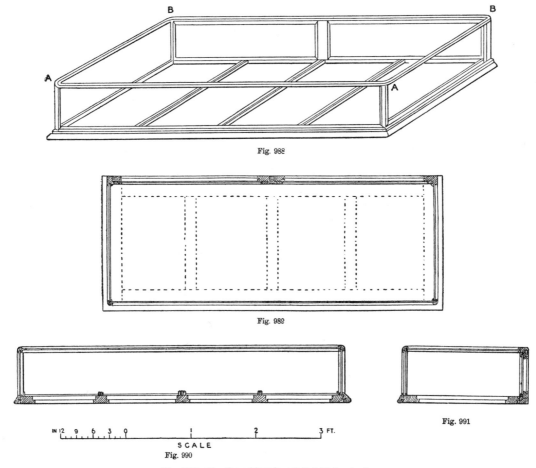

Figs. 988 to 991.—General Drawings of Airtight Counter-Case

Fig. 988, Isometrical projection; fig. 989, plan; fig. 990, longitudinal section; fig. 991, transverse section

ness of the moulding on the front edge and $1\frac{1}{2}$ inch for a hardwood slip on the back edge of the frame (see fig. 992). The length will be the extreme length of the case *minus* two thicknesses of moulding.

Mortise and tenon the frame together, and rebate it to receive $\frac{5}{8}$-inch panels flush on the inside; then glue up and take to size. The hardwood slip can now be jointed and glued on, a tongued and grooved joint being used for this purpose. After this has been done, the airtight rebate to receive the doors should be worked on the hardwood slip. In order to make a good job of the rebate, it will be necessary to have a special plane for working both the rebate and the small half-round tongue at one time.

To complete the bottom, groove the front edge and both ends for the tongue, then mitre and fix the moulding to the frame. The moulding must be specially noted. It must project above the bottom $\frac{3}{16}$ inch to form a rebate for the glass; and the first member, *i.e.* the part projecting, must be rounded to intersect with the upright angle-bars (figs. 992–993), which mitre into the moulding.

The panels in the bottom are to be screwed to the frame. Before putting the whole case together, they must be taken out for enabling the small fillets which secure the glass to be easily screwed into their respective positions.

Framework for Glass.—Plane up the stuff for the round angle-bars, gauging it to $\frac{9}{16}$ inch square, and rebate $\frac{1}{8}$ inch deep and $\frac{1}{8}$ inch from the face-edges. The angle-bars will then appear as seen in fig. 995. For the back part of the frame, square up the stuff to $1\frac{1}{2}$ inch by $\frac{3}{4}$ inch, and rebate $\frac{1}{4}$ inch deep and $\frac{1}{8}$ inch from the face for the glass. For the doors, take out the rebate $\frac{1}{4}$ inch deep by $\frac{5}{8}$ inch wide; bevel the rebate to $\frac{5}{16}$ inch deep on

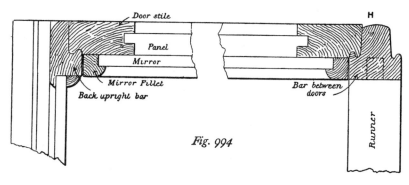

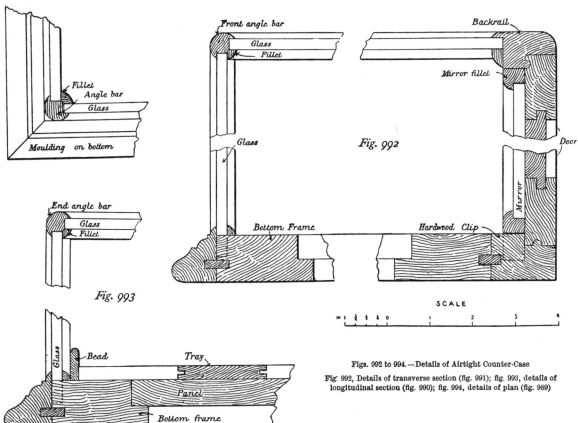

Figs. 992 to 994.—Details of Airtight Counter-Case

Fig. 992, Details of transverse section (fig. 991); fig. 993, details of longitudinal section (fig. 990); fig. 994, details of plan (fig. 989)

the outside edge (as shown in fig. 996), and work the hook-joint plane on the edge of the rebate. It is best to make the mitred joints first, as they require careful fitting together, and the bottom ends can afterwards be easily taken to the required length and cut.

Fig. 998 contains isometrical projections showing the joints at the intersection of the front and the end angle-bars with the upright angle-bar. The position of the joint is shown at A, fig. 988.

Three pieces of the required section (fig. 995) should be got out, and the joint worked as follows:—

Commence with the front and end angle-bars, cutting a square mitre (45°) on each outside face of both bars, bringing the external angle to a point, as shown in the sketch.

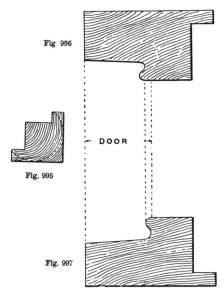

Fig. 996

DOOR

Fig. 995

Fig. 997

Figs. 995 to 997.—Full-size Details of Airtight Counter-Case

Fig. 995, Section of angle-bars; fig. 996, section of
back upright bar; fig. 997, section of back rail

Cut the mitre down to the rebate line and cut the surplus away, leaving the core of the bar projecting, which will be the part c. The internal part of the mitre E is the sight-line. Square down and across the core; then, from the sight-line, measure distances of $\frac{1}{8}$ inch and $\frac{7}{16}$ inch; the resulting lines will be the shoulder and end of the dovetail respectively. Cut the core off at the longest line and form the dovetail as shown in the sketch, when the two bars can be fitted together.

Proceed with the upright angle-bar. Cut the square mitre as before, but instead of cutting to the depth of the rebate, it must be cut $\frac{1}{32}$ inch less. From the sight-line F measure the same distances as before, viz. $\frac{1}{8}$ inch and $\frac{7}{16}$ inch. Cut off at the longest line, taking care not to cut through the projecting point of the mitre, then take out the core c back to the shoulder line, thus leaving a thin tenon as seen in the sketch. Cut the tenon back $\frac{1}{16}$ inch on each edge and continue the mitre through.

It will now be necessary to mortise the front and end bars to receive the tenon on the upright angle-bar. For the mortise, square a line across the mitre $\frac{1}{16}$ inch from the sight-line E. Gauge a line down the mitre $\frac{3}{32}$ inch from the face

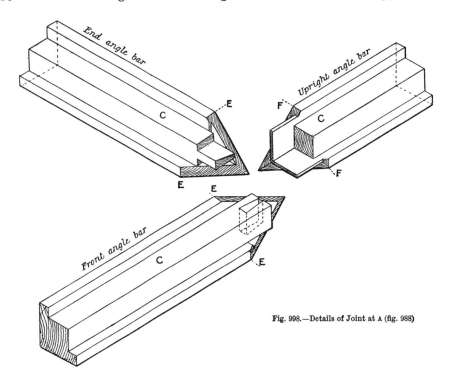

End angle bar

Upright angle bar

Front angle bar

Fig. 998.—Details of Joint at A (fig. 988)

of the bar, leaving $\frac{1}{32}$ inch (the width of the mortise) between the core of the bar and the gauge-line. The depth of the mortise will be to within $\frac{1}{8}$ inch from the other face.

The work must be done very carefully, and great care taken to have the tenon on the upright angle-bar of the thickness stated, viz. $\frac{1}{32}$ inch, as the result of having it of greater thickness would be that, when the bars were rounded, it would work through to the face.

The front angle-bar will have the same joint on both ends. The joint at the back of the case on the end angle-bar is cut as shown at fig. 999. The joint at the bottom end of each upright angle-bar is simply a square shoulder cut to the depth of the rebate, leaving the core of the bar projecting to form a stump tenon. The bars are afterwards mitred with the moulding on both the front and the end, the projecting round of the moulding being

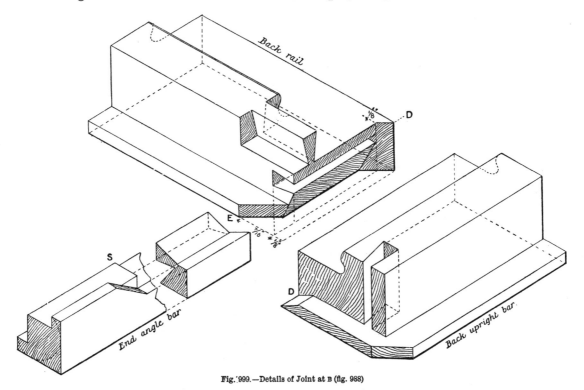

Fig. 999.—Details of Joint at B (fig. 988)

cut away between the mitres in order to allow the shoulder to butt on the first square member, which will be flush with the bottom.

Fig. 999 contains isometrical projections showing the joints used to unite the back rail with the back upright angle-bar for forming the door opening: and also the end angle-bar. The position of the joint will be clearly understood by referring to B, fig. 988.

It will be well to follow the same system as in the last group of joints, i.e. to prepare a piece of the required section of back rail (fig. 996) which, when cut into two parts, can be used for both the back rail and the back angle-bar; the only difference in the section of the two being that the back rail is rebated $\frac{1}{16}$ inch less than the thickness of the doors instead of $\frac{1}{8}$ inch less as in the back upright bar (fig. 997). The reason for this is so as to allow the round of the hook-joint on the back upright bar to project over the hook-joint on the back rail which butts against it. It also allows a continuous hollow on the edges of the doors, which would not be the case if the rebates were kept flush with each other.

The end angle-bar is dovetailed into the back rail, and is also mitred both at the extreme end and at the rebate. Fig. 1000 shows the plan of this joint. It will be observed that the joint has been left open to show the bevel from the shoulder line to the dovetail on the back rail, as at A, fig. 1002.

The back rail is also dovetailed to receive the upright bar. If the reader will look at fig. 999, and imagine the upright placed into position on the back rail, he will notice that D, D meet and form the remaining part of the mitre, leaving a shoulder and mitre to join the end angle-bar when in position. The exact position of the latter is seen in fig. 1001, the dotted lines showing the position of the dovetail on the back rail.

We will now proceed to set out the work.

Commencing with the end angle-bar, square off a line for the extreme end of the mitre at B, fig. 1000, and measure back the width of the back rail (namely $1\frac{1}{2}$ inch) to C, which will be the sight-line. From the sight-line set off $\frac{5}{16}$ inch for the shoulder of the dovetail as at S, figs. 999 and 1000; then set off $1\frac{3}{8}$ inch from the sight-line to the end of the dovetail. Set a gauge to the centre of the angle-bar for the shoulders, as at D, figs. 1000 and 1001. The

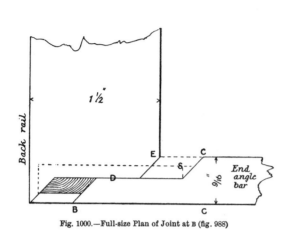

Fig. 1000.—Full-size Plan of Joint at B (fig. 988)

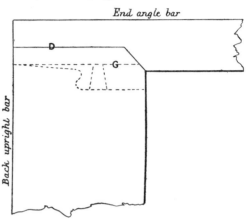

Fig. 1001.—Full-size End Elevation of Joint at B (fig. 988)

shoulder at D (fig. 1000) is cut under on the bevel as shown in the section through the joint at A, fig. 1002, and in the sketch of the end angle-bar (fig. 999) where the drawing is broken. It is necessary to bevel it in this way in order to obtain the requisite strength in the dovetail. The shoulder on the side (fig. 1001) is cut square as shown in the sketch. Mark the mitres, cutting from the sight-line to the shoulder-line. The mitre on the extreme end is cut through as shown in fig. 1000.

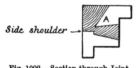

Side shoulder →

Fig. 1002.—Section through Joint of End Angle-Bar (fig. 999)

To set out the back rail as shown in fig. 999, square a line for the extreme end of the mitre, and from this line measure back for the sight-line, namely, $\frac{9}{16}$ inch, the width of the angle-bar, as at E, fig. 1000. Square a line between the two lines obtained, at an equal distance from each, for the shoulder D. From E measure $\frac{7}{16}$ inch towards the end of the bar, and cut off square to within $\frac{1}{8}$ inch of the outside edge; this is clearly shown in fig. 999.

To mark the dovetail of the end angle-bar, make a thin hardwood or zinc pattern to fit the dovetail on the angle-bar, and apply it to the rebate of the back rail, cutting the dovetail out very carefully to within $\frac{1}{8}$ inch of the outside edge. On the top side of the rail mark the external mitre from the extreme point to the shoulder-line, and cut as shown in figs. 999 and 1000. Before the mitre can be completed, the bevel must be cut along the shoulder-line and edge of dovetail, and must work out against the mitre. The internal mitre is cut from the sight-line.

There now only remains the cutting of the dovetail to receive the upright bar. Referring to fig. 999, it will be seen that it is necessary to obtain the shoulder-line only, which is accomplished by measuring from the extreme point of the mitre (D, fig. 999) $\frac{3}{4}$ inch, the thickness of the upright bar. The position of the dovetail-joint between the back rail and the back upright bar is shown by the dotted lines in fig. 1001.

The exact lines for setting out the back upright bar (see fig. 1001) are found as follows:—Square the shoulder-line D and set off for the back shoulder $\frac{1}{4}$ inch as shown by the dotted line G. The back shoulder is then cut off to within $\frac{1}{8}$ inch of the face, as in the sketch, fig. 999. Make a pattern to fit the dovetail on the back rail, and apply it to the back of the bar. Mitre the $\frac{1}{4}$-inch projection on the outside edge, and also mitre the inside as shown.

It is absolutely necessary that the whole of this work should be executed very carefully and very neatly. When the above-mentioned joints have been fitted, take the bars to the required length.

To set out the bottom end of the back upright bar, cut the face-shoulder square and mitre with the moulding as previously described for the front angle-bar. Allow the back-shoulder to be $\frac{1}{4}$ inch longer, so as to fit in the rebate for the doors, the tenon being in the position shown by the dotted lines in fig. 992.

After all the joints have been made, round the angle-bars and the back rail. The external angles of all upright angle-bars must have the rounding turned out about $\frac{1}{2}$ inch above the bottom shoulder, leaving the bottom part of the bar square to follow the line of the moulding. The joints can now be glued together and cleaned off.

The double-rebated upright bar between the doors (as at H, fig. 994) is cut to fit both the top and bottom rebate, a small dovetail being cut at both ends in the positions shown by the dotted lines. The front edge of the bar is slightly rounded to break the joint between the doors. From the inside of the bar a runner of the same thickness as the bar is screwed to the bottom of the case, to keep the trays in position.

Doors.—There is nothing special to note in framing up the doors; they may be either tenoned or dowelled together. The panel is prepared flush on the inside.

Carefully fit the doors to the opening, and work the hook-joint on the top edge and both ends. It will be remembered that the hook-joint must be worked through on each end; and also that it is deeper than the hook-joint on the top rail. In working the small hollow to fit over the fillet on the bottom edge, work the plane from the back side of the door.

Hinge the doors on the bottom edge, fixing the butts against the outside edge of the half-round fillet. When fixed thus the airtight joint will remain intact. The doors are fastened by a spring catch or lock let into the top rail.

When the doors are hung, the position of the mirror fillet can be marked by lining down the back of the doors round the frame. The fillets should be fixed $\frac{1}{32}$ inch inside the lines to allow for clearing.

Trays.—A cross section of the tray is shown in fig. 993. The bottom is prepared from three pieces of $\frac{1}{4}$-inch pine. The grain of the centre piece runs from back to front of the case, the grain of the side pieces being at right angles to it; and the three pieces are tongued and grooved together as shown. Glue the pieces together, and, when set, mitre the bead round the bottom.

Another method of ensuring the bottom against warping is to have the bottom in three thicknesses, the grain of the centre piece crossing the grain of the two outside pieces, and the pieces being glued together.

The inside of the tray and over the bead are covered with velvet or some other material which must be glued to the tray. Glue should be used sparingly so as to prevent it penetrating the material.

3. CIRCULAR-FRONTED COUNTER-CASE WITH GLASS ENDS

Fig. 1003 shows a cross section through a circular-fronted case with glass ends. The only difference in the construction of this case from that of the square case is the bent angle-bar, and, of course, the omission of a front angle-bar.

In making this case it is first necessary to have the glass bent to the shape required. For this purpose a pattern of the curve should be sent to a glass manufacturer. When the glass has been received, make a mould of the same shape, on which to bend the angle-bar, as shown in fig. 1004. The convex side of the glass will give the rebate line from which to work the mould.

Use birch for the angle-bar as it bends easily; it can be stained to match the other part of the case. Have the bar long enough to bend from the bottom of the case to the back rail.

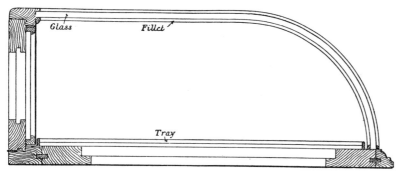

Fig. 1003.—Transverse Section of Circular-fronted Counter-Case with Glass Ends

To bend the bar successfully, cut the top side of the bar away down to the rebate line on the end required to be bent. The length of the part cut away will be from the bottom of the case to a little beyond the springing line. Care must be taken to cut the two bars for the case in pairs. Steam the bars for several hours and then bend them round the mould (fig. 1004) by securing the extreme end first with a cleat, as shown at A. Draw the bar gradually to the mould, secure it in position by the cleat B, and leave it to cool for several hours. It

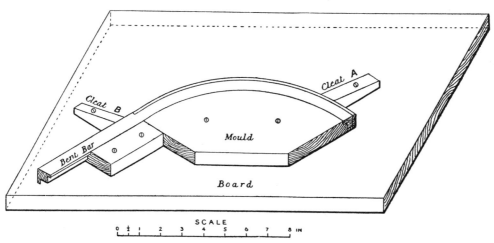

Fig. 1004.—Method of Bending the Angle-Bars

is better to leave it on the mould until the following day, when the strip to form the rebate —which replaces the part cut away—can be fitted and glued in position.

After the bar has been bent, and the strip cleaned off, place it on the drawing-board, and set out the position of the joints at the bottom of the case and on the back rail, as already described.

4. CIRCULAR-FRONTED CASE WITH SOLID ENDS

It will only be necessary, after the preceding explanations, to notice the joint of the back rail, and the section of the solid end. Fig. 1005 shows a section through the solid end of the case, grooved to receive the glass. Fig. 1006 is a plan of the angle formed by the end of the case and the back rail. The clamp A is tongued and grooved to the end, the tongue being stopped $\frac{1}{2}$ inch below the top edge. The clamp is prepared with a hook-joint as shown by the dotted lines. The width of the clamp is the width of the back rail less the rebate for glass.

Fig. 1007 shows in isometrical projection the joint at the junction of the back rail with the solid end.   Imagine that A A are brought together.   It will then be seen that they slide into position and present the appearance shown on the plan in fig. 1006, and give the exact lines for setting out the work.

The solid ends are $\frac{5}{8}$ inch thick, finished size. They must be left wide enough to screw

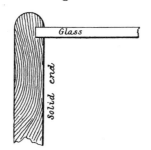

Fig. 1005.—Section of Solid End grooved for Glass

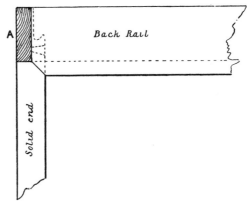

Fig. 1006.—Plan of Joint between Solid End and Back Rail

to the bottom frame of the case.   Fix the moulding round the bottom, and mitre it at each inside round of the ends, as before described for upright angle-bars, turning the round on the outside of each end out $\frac{1}{2}$ inch above the moulding. The moulding mitred round

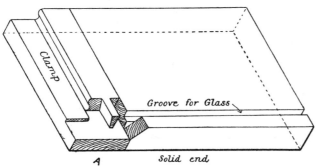

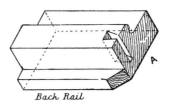

Fig. 1007.—Isometrical Projection of Joint between Solid End and Back Rail

the ends of the case must be reduced by the thickness of the quarter-round member which forms the rebate for glass at the front of the case.

These cases are often fitted with several trays, the bearers to carry them being screwed to the ends.

Part II.—WOOD-TURNING

By R. W. COLE, B.A.

CHAPTER I

PLAIN TURNING

Introductory.—Turning in wood is of two kinds—simple and ornamental. In the former, pieces of wood are moulded by tools into such shapes that any cross section at right angles to the length is a circle; in the latter, the cross section is of irregular shape. A plain lathe of the simplest description is used for plain turning, but ornamental turning requires several additional appliances which are mounted on the ordinary lathe.

Description of Lathe.—Lathes suitable for wood-turning are of many sizes and different designs. As plain turning does not require any elaborate or accurate machinery, the lathes used in wood-working shops are generally of the roughest description. The principle of all lathes is the same. A lathe very suitable for wood-turning is shown in fig. 1008, where A A is the bed, B B the standards, which are firmly bolted to each end of the bed, C the crank-shaft, and D the crank, which is connected to the treadle, F, by the crank-pin, E. The crank-shaft is pivoted to the standards at each end, and a driving-wheel, G, is keyed close to the left-hand end. The head-stock, H, is bolted to the left-hand end of the bed. Inside this the mandrel, I, with the pulley-wheel, J, is fixed so that the screwed end of the former projects about 1 inch over the bed. The hand-rest, K, slides along the bed, and can be fastened in any position by screwing up a handle underneath. The T-rest, L, is fastened into the top of the rest so that it can be turned round and fixed in any position. It is called the "rest" because the tools which are used for turning are held on to it by the hand. The back-poppet or back-centre, M, can also slide along the bed and be fastened in any position. By turning the wheel, N, a cylindrical piece of steel, O, pointed at one end, can be pushed out of the back-poppet or drawn into it. This piece of steel, and another of the same shape which can be screwed on to the right-hand end of the mandrel, are called the "centres" of the lathe. Three or more grooves are

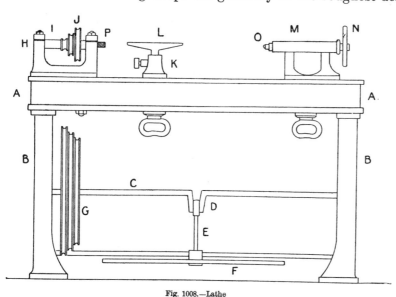

Fig. 1008.—Lathe

turned on the fly-wheel and mandrel-pulley, so that they can be connected with a gut or leather belt for imparting motion from the former to the latter. If the grooves at the left-hand edge of the two wheels are connected by a belt, higher speed is obtained than when the others are connected.

The size of a lathe is measured by the length of its bed and the height of the centre of the mandrel from the top of the bed; for instance, if this height is 6 inches, the lathe would be said to be of 6 inches centre. A gap-bed lathe is one the bed of which is bent down in the shape of a U for about a foot on the right-hand side of the headstock. This is to allow an object of large diameter, such as a table-top or wheel, to be turned.

Appliances.—Instruments called "chucks" are used to mount the wood to be turned on the lathe. These are shown in fig. 1009, where A is a cup chuck, B a fork chuck, C a

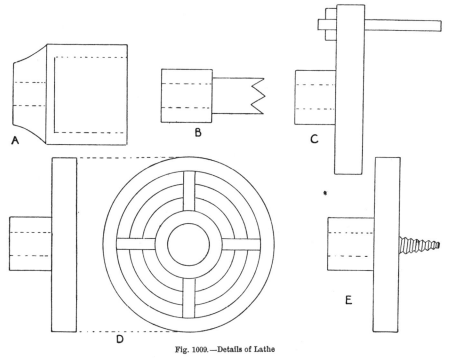

Fig. 1009.—Details of Lathe

A, Cup chuck; B, fork chuck; C, driver; D, face-plate; E, flange chuck

driver, D a face-plate, and E a flange chuck. All these chucks are tapped with female screws at the left-hand end, so that they can screw on to the projecting end of the mandrel. The cup chuck is used for holding wood which is to be bored out, one end of the wood being pared down and hammered into it. The fork chuck and driver are used when long pieces of wood are mounted between the centres, as in making table-legs. The flange chuck is for turning circular discs of wood, a hole being bored in the centre of the wood so that it can be screwed on to the taper-screw. The face-plate is used for the same purpose, or for holding large blocks which are to be bored, such blocks being fastened on with ordinary screws or with iron clamps. For chucking articles of special shape, such as rings, a block of wood can be screwed to the mandrel and turned down to the right size. There is another chuck, known as the self-centring chuck, in which three jaws moved by turning a key grasp the material to be turned.

Turning Tools.—The tools used for plain turning are shown in fig. 1010, where A is a gouge, B a double-bevel chisel, C a side-boring chisel, D a parting tool, E a round tool, F a bent chisel, G a half-round tool, H a hook tool, I and J outside and inside screwing tools, and K a pair of callipers. Double-bevel chisels, thin gouges, and hook tools are for soft woods only; all the rest are used for hard woods. The gouge is used for taking the rough off the wood and reducing it to a circular shape, when, if soft, it is moulded into the required shape by a double-bevel chisel.   The hook tool is for boring soft wood; the side-boring tool and bent chisel are for boring hard wood.   The parting tool is for cutting off the finished article from the remainder of the wood.   The round tool is for moulding the interior,

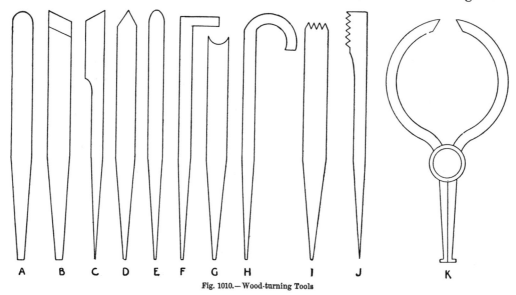

Fig. 1010.—Wood-turning Tools

and the half-round tool for making rings on the exterior or for making small balls.   The callipers are for taking the diameter of articles whilst being turned.

The Slide-rest.—Fig. 1011 represents the slide-rest, which is used for turning hard woods when the tool is to be held firmly.   It is necessary for copying with templates, also for ornamental turning.   The tool is clamped into a piece of steel, A, and this can be made

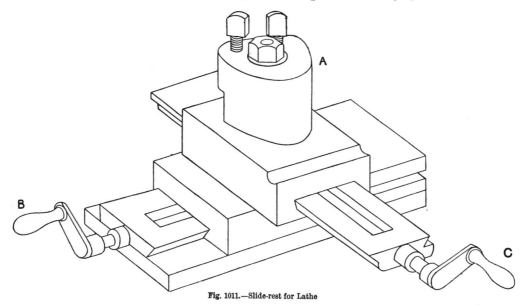

Fig. 1011.—Slide-rest for Lathe

to move in transverse direction by turning the handle, B, which works a slide, or in a direction at right angles to the lathe-bed by turning a similar handle, C.   In some slide-rests the upper part can swivel round, and the tool be thus moved along a line inclined at any angle to the bed.   This is useful in turning cones having a required angle.

Woods.—The woods used for turning are roughly divided into *hard* and *soft*,[1] each of

---

[1] This rough classification of turners' woods must not be confounded with the general classification of timber into "hard woods" and "soft woods".

these kinds requiring different treatment. Amongst the former are box, ebony, green ebony, cocus, kingwood, cam, lignum-vitæ, rosewood, tulip, olive, satin, &c. The latter include walnut, mahogany, oak, beech, ash, chestnut, holly, laurel, acacia, laburnum, elm, lime, sycamore, deal, pine, willow, cherry, plum, pear, and apple. Box is the cheapest of the harder woods, and is suitable for the most delicate ornamentation. Ebony is very brittle, hence it is not suitable for fine work. Green ebony has a slightly greenish tinge, and resembles ebony in turning qualities. Cocus is a dark-brown wood with whitish markings, kingwood is streaked with crimson and dark-brown, camwood is of a dark-red colour, lignum vitæ is dark-green mixed with yellow, rosewood is dark-red, and tulip-wood is of a yellow colour with crimson markings. All these woods are of nearly the same degree of hardness, and are used for turning small fancy articles. Olive-wood and satin-wood are softer than the majority of hard woods; the former is brownish-yellow, the latter is bright yellow with beautiful markings.

The soft woods are too well known to require individual description. Oak, walnut, and mahogany are used for making balusters, newels, curtain-poles, table-legs, and other parts of furniture. Beech and ash are principally used for tool-handles, whilst sycamore, chestnut, deal, and pine are used for household turnery and cheap furniture. Parts of chairs are generally made of cherry, which is rather a brittle wood. The woods of other fruit-trees, such as apple, plum, damson, and pear, are very handsomely marked; so also are acacia, laburnum, laurel, and lilac. Holly-wood is of a pure white colour and turns well, but it is difficult to obtain.

In turning the harder woods, tools with short bevels are used; but tools for the softer woods have much longer bevels, and the speed of the lathe is very high.

Mounting Wood on Lathe.—When the article to be turned is not hollow, the wood is mounted between the centres; that is to say, holes are bored at either end, the prong of the fork chuck is fitted into one and the back-centre is screwed up into the other. Articles of

almost any length may be turned, but the proportion of length to diameter must not exceed a certain maximum, which depends on the nature of the wood. If this maximum is exceeded, the wood will vibrate while it is being turned, and the surface will be left rough. When hollow articles are to be turned, the wood is secured only to the mandrel-centre. It is either hammered into a cup chuck or screwed to a face-plate, so that the right-hand end projects over the lathe-bed, and can be bored out to the right depth by tools held on the **T**-rest. In turning flat articles, such as table-tops or bread-platters, a piece of board is roughly cut with a saw to the right size, and either screwed on to the face-plate or flange chuck. Large table-tops

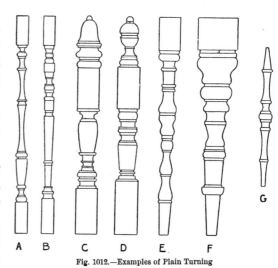

Fig. 1012.—Examples of Plain Turning

can be turned by using a lathe with a gap-bed, or turning the mandrel round so that the wood swings over the left-hand end of the bed.

Examples of Plain Turning.—Some examples of plain turning between the centres are shown in fig. 1012, where A and B are balusters, C and D newels, E and F table-legs, and G a chair-rail. All these articles are turned from strips of wood which have been sawn from a plank and planed so that the cross-section is approximately square. The parts which are not turned can be left square or turned to a plain circular shape. A variety of patterns can be obtained by turning pieces of wood of triangular, hexagonal, or octagonal section. When a piece of work composed of several parts is turned, the various parts are fixed together by circular tenons and mortises. The former are turned when the work is on the lathe, the latter are bored subsequently.

Inlaying.—Inlaying consists in letting in several concentric rings of different woods, or spots of different woods, into flat surfaces, such as table-tops. In the former kind, the portion of the article to be inlayed is bored out to $\frac{1}{4}$ inch in depth, and a plug of another kind of wood is turned to fit this, and glued in. When dry, this plug is bored out until a ring of the requisite width is left. Another plug is glued into this, and the process repeated until the required number of rings has been inlayed. In spot inlaying, shallow holes are bored in the article to form a certain pattern, and these are filled with circular plugs of different woods.

Turning Balls.—Balls are turned by a spherical rest, which is a kind of slide-rest in which the point of the tool is made to describe a semicircle of variable diameter, thus cutting out a sphere. Balls can also be turned quite accurately by hand by a skilled operator, and this is how billiard balls are usually made.

Square Turning.—Square turning is the name given to the process of turning balusters and other articles, so that a section at right angles to the length is nearly square. Square

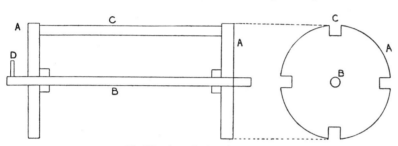

Fig. 1013.—Apparatus for Square Turning

lengths of wood cut to the required size are fastened into a piece of apparatus which can be mounted between the lathe centres. Side and end views of this apparatus are shown in fig. 1013. Two circular discs of wood, A A, about 8 inches in diameter, slide along a circular iron bar, B, and can be fastened at any distance apart. Four equidistant notches are cut on the circumference of both, and into these the ends of the pieces of wood to be turned are fixed. One such piece of wood is shown in position at C. A piece of projecting metal, D, catches in the driver chuck, thus causing the instrument to revolve. The pattern is first cut on the outer surface of each piece of wood, then they are turned round, and fresh surfaces exposed and turned to the same pattern, the process being repeated until the four surfaces are turned. A template and slide-rest are usually necessary to get the patterns on each surface exactly the same. The surfaces turned in this manner will be slightly curved, but by increasing the diameter of the discs, A A, the curvature can be diminished. Triangular or hexagonal pieces of wood can be turned in the same manner.

Copying.—Copies of turned work are almost always executed by hand, but they can also be done by a slide-rest and template.

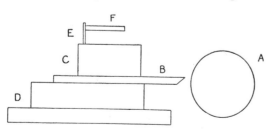

Fig. 1014.—Apparatus for Copying Turnery

A longitudinal section of the object to be copied is drawn on paper, this section extending from the axis to the turned edge. The section is then cut out on a thin strip of metal or hard wood. The pattern thus formed is called a template. It is attached to a framework which is fixed to the lathe-bed over the slide-rest, and adjusted so that it just clears the latter. A steel rod about $\frac{1}{8}$ inch in diameter is fixed to the top of the slide-rest, and rubs against the curved edge of the template. A sectional view of the arrangement is shown in fig. 1014, A being the wood, B the turning tool held in the tool-holder, C, of the slide-rest, D, and E the steel rod resting against the template, F. If the steel rod is moved along the edge of the template by turning the slide-rest handles, the tool will cut a corresponding pattern on the wood.

The Elliptic Chuck.—The elliptic chuck is used for turning objects of elliptical section. It consists of two parts, a frame bent twice at right angles and the chuck proper. The former is fastened across the right-hand end of the headstock with thumb-screws. A circular ring projects about 1 inch from the frame, and encircles the screwed end of the mandrel. The chuck proper is somewhat similar to the eccentric chuck, there being a frame which screws on to the mandrel, a slide, a divided disc, and a spring catch. There is no screw attached to the slide, but it is free to move backwards and forwards. Two jaws are attached to the slide; these pass through slots cut in the frame. If the ring is concentric with the mandrel, the usual rotary motion will be imparted to the chuck when the lathe works. But if the ring is moved from its concentric position by loosening one screw of the frame and tightening the other, the motion will be elliptical. The eccentricity of the ellipse is increased or diminished by moving the ring from or towards its concentric position.

The Eccentric Chuck.—The eccentric chuck is used for ornamenting turned articles with a series of eccentric circles. Fig. 1015 is an illustration of the form of eccentric chuck manufactured by the Britannia Company. It consists of a base-plate, A, with a screwed boss for attaching it to the mandrel of the lathe. A slide, B, is worked between guides fastened to the base-plate by turning a screw the end of which projects at D. A divided head, E, is also fastened to the end of the screw. A divided circular plate is attached to the front of the slide, and can be turned by a tangent screw, which is made to revolve by attaching a key to its squared edge, H. Another screw, similar in size and pitch to the mandrel screw, is attached to the centre of the divided plate and receives a cup chuck. A pin, K, is inserted into the slide to hold it to the base-plate and take off the strain when the wood is being turned.

Fig. 1015.—Eccentric Chuck

The eccentric chuck enables the turner to bring almost any point on the surface of a flat disc into the axial line of the mandrel, hence making it for the time being the centre about which the work revolves. When the slide is screwed right into the base-plate, the wood revolves about its centre, but as the slide is screwed out, it revolves about a centre which is gradually removed from its own. A tool held in the slide-rest will cut a circle which is more or less eccentric to the wood held in the chuck. If the divided plate is turned round into different positions by the ratchet, a series of interlacing circles will be cut on the surface of the wood.

CHAPTER II

ORNAMENTAL TURNING

Fluting and Drill Work.—The same kind of lathe is used for fluting and other kinds of ornamental turning, but it is fitted with additional appliances, such as division-plate and index, overhead motion, and drilling and cutting instruments.

The division-plate consists of a circular brass plate fixed to the right-hand side of the mandrel pulley. Four or five concentric circles of holes are bored on the surface of this plate, there being 360 in the outer circle, 112 in the next, 96 in the third, 78 in the next, and 42 in the innermost. The index is a steel point attached to the end of a spring which is fastened to the headstock, so that it can project over either circle of holes. It is used for holding the mandrel in any position by allowing it to catch in any one of the holes. By its aid the surface of a piece of wood can be divided into 360, 112, 96, 78, or 42 parts, or into any number of parts which is a factor of these numbers.

The overhead apparatus is shown in fig. 1016. Two upright iron pillars, A A, are fastened at either end of the lathe-bed, B B. A pulley, D, and a roller, E, are fastened to

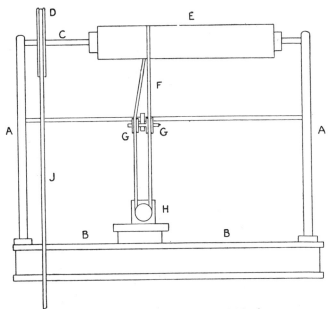

Fig. 1016.—Overhead Apparatus for Ornamental Turning

an axis, C, which is pivoted on the uprights. A gut-band, F, passes over the roller, two guide-pulleys, G G, and the pulley, H, which is connected with the drilling instrument. The guide-pulleys are attached to one end of a lever, and a weight is fastened to the other end to keep the gut-band tight. The drilling instrument is held in the slide-rest so that it can be moved in a direction along or at right angles to the bed. The usual belt is taken off the mandrel-pulley, and the pulley, D, is connected with the driving-wheel by a belt, J. It will thus be seen that a slow motion of the treadle will impart a very rapid motion to the drill.

Fig. 1017 is an illustration of the drilling instrument. It consists of a hollow iron stem, A, in which a spindle, B, rotates. A pulley, C, is attached to one end of the spindle, and the other is bored to receive the drill, D. Several of these drills of different sizes and shapes are necessary for ornamental turning.

If it is required to flute a cylinder, a piece of wood is mounted between the centres and turned in the usual manner. If, for example, 20 flutes are to be cut, the circle of the division-plate which contains 360 divisions is used. The index is fastened into the zero, and a suitable drill made to revolve and worked up and down the wood, by turning the handles of the slide-rest, until a flute of the right depth has been cut. Stops are fastened to

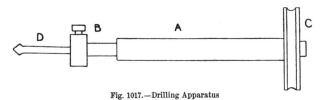

Fig. 1017.—Drilling Apparatus

the slide-rest to prevent the drill cutting too deep. The division-plate is then turned 18 divisions and another flute cut, and so on, until all the flutes have been cut. The edges of the flutes can be made to meet or not by using drills of the right size. The shape of the flute depends on the shape of the edge of the drill. Step-shaped flutes can be cut by first cutting to a certain depth with a narrow drill, then not quite so deep with another and wider drill. A curved surface can be fluted by using a template to guide the drilling instrument.

Another kind of ornamental turning is effected by drilling a series of holes on the surface of turned articles with drills the edges of which are ground to different shapes. The holes are properly spaced by using the division-plate and holding the drilling instrument in the slide-rest. Some ornamental drills are shown in fig. 1018; A is used for drilling holes or fluting, B and C for drilling holes only, D will cut a **V**-shaped flute or drill tapering holes, E will cut a step-shaped flute, and F will only bore holes. Trifolia and other patterns can be cut by properly spacing the holes. Turned articles can be ornamented by a combination of fluting and drill-work.

The Eccentric Cutter.—The eccentric cutter is one of a variety of drilling instruments which are used for executing drill-work in a manner similar to that already described. They are all held in the slide-rest, and worked by a belt which hangs down from the

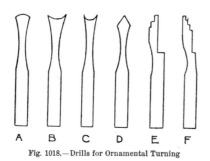

Fig. 1018.—Drills for Ornamental Turning

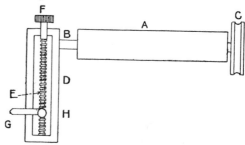

Fig. 1019.—Eccentric Cutter

overhead motion. Fig. 1019 is an illustration of the eccentric cutter; it consists of a square piece of steel, A, down the centre of which a hole is bored. A steel spindle, B, fits into this hole, a pulley, C, is fixed to the end which projects at the right hand, and a frame, D, is fastened to the other end. A screw, E, is worked inside this frame by turning the milled head, F. A drill or cutter, G, is attached to the screw by a nut. When the milled head is turned, the cutter is worked towards or away from the centre of the spindle. If the cutter is at the centre of the spindle, it will bore a simple hole, but if the screw is turned, it will move away from the centre and cut a circle. The appearance of such a circle can be varied by using drills with differently-shaped edges. By using the division-plate and index, combinations of circles similar to those cut with the aid of the eccentric chuck can be obtained.

The Vertical Cutter.—Fig. 1020 is an illustration of the vertical cutter. It consists of a frame of steel, A B, attached to a shank, C, which is held in the slide-rest. A spindle, D, revolves in the frame, and is worked by a belt which passes over the pulley, E. The cutter, F, is attached to the spindle by a screw. The frame is fixed in the rest so that the cutter rotates in a vertical plane, but some instruments are made so that the frame can be twisted into any position by loosening a screw at the right-hand end of the shank, thus making the cutter revolve in a plane which may be inclined at any angle to the vertical. If the instrument is held in one position, it will scoop out a hole in the wood, the shape of the hole depending on the curve of the edge of the drill. This cutter is used with the division-plate in the same manner as the eccentric cutter.

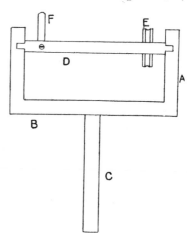

Fig. 1020.—Vertical Cutter

The Horizontal Cutter.—The horizontal cutter is similar to the vertical cutter, but the tool revolves in a horizontal plane.

The Universal Cutter.—The universal cutter can be set in a vertical or horizontal position, or in any position between the two.

The Elliptic Cutter.—The elliptic cutter is used for cutting ellipses on turned work. The eccentricity of the ellipse and its size are adjusted by turning two screws. Ellipses can be combined together to form complicated patterns by using the division-plate.

The Rose Cutter.—The rose cutter is an instrument which causes the axis of the cutting

drill to receive a rotary and oscillating motion simultaneously.   A small steel roller attached
to a slide is kept in contact with a rosette by a spring, and causes the tool to follow the
curves of the latter when the cutter is set in motion.   Different patterns can be cut by using
rosettes of different shapes.   Very beautiful effects are obtained by using the instrument
with the division-plate.

Combination Ornamental Apparatus.—Fig. 1021 is an illustration of a combined epicycloidal, rose-cutting, eccentric-cutting, drilling, fluting, and vertical-cutting apparatus
manufactured by the Britannia Company of Colchester.   It is a cheap and efficient
instrument, performing a great variety of ornamental work which could hitherto only be
executed by a number of expensive instruments.   It can be used on any lathe provided with
a slide-rest and scroll chuck; the only extra fittings required are a wheel attached to the
chuck and a movable bracket bolted to the headstock.   The engraving shows the apparatus

Fig. 1021.—Combined Epicycloidal, Rose-cutting, Eccentric-cutting, Drilling, Fluting, and Vertical-cutting Apparatus

attached to an ordinary lathe; T is the slide-rest in which is clamped the frame L L', carrying
a revolving spindle.   The wheel D is attached to the spindle by a set-screw, the boss being
to the left and close to the frame, which prevents the spindle from moving to the right or left.
This wheel is connected by the wheel C, on shaft G, by means of the carrier wheels X X,
fitted to the frame E, which is fixed in any desired position by means of the screw and nut
on the adjustable arm Q.   This arm is centred on one of the steel collars in which the
spindle carrying the tool works, so that in whatever position it is fixed the carrier wheels
always remain in gear with wheel D.   They can also by the arm R be kept in gear with C, so
that by slacking the set-screw which retains the arm Q in any desired position, the slide-rest
may be advanced to or from the work V to be ornamented, all the wheels remaining in gear.
The shaft G is supported on the right by the pillar H fixed in the socket of the hand-rest S,
and on the left by a bracket I attached by a set-screw.   The shaft is connected by a wheel B
with the wheel A, which is fastened to the chuck U.

A spiral may be cut by this apparatus by using the vertical cutter rotated by the
overhead motion.   The bracket I is bolted to the front of the headstock, and the hand-rest
containing the pillar H is brought forward so that the shaft G is in front of the wood.   A
collar is fastened to the slide-rest and centred on the handle, and on this collar the arm Q
works, the carrier wheels being bolted on the right-hand side instead of the left.   These
wheels gear with a small wheel fixed on the handle of the rest, and with the wheel C on
shaft G.   The spirals are varied by using wheels of different sizes.

Turning Spirals.—A spiral is cut on a cylinder of wood in a manner similar to that in which screws are cut on metal by self-acting lathes. As the mandrel of the lathe revolves, it imparts its motion to a series of cog-wheels called change-wheels. A long steel shaft, with a screw cut on its surface, extends underneath the bed from one end to the other. This is called the leading screw. The slide-rest is attached to it by a nut, so that when it revolves the slide is moved along the bed. The end of the leading screw under the headstock is attached to a cog-wheel which is rotated by the change-wheels. Thus, when the mandrel revolves, a traversing motion along the lathe-bed is imparted to the slide-rest, and a tool held in it would cut a screw upon a piece of wood mounted between the centres. The pitch of the screw depends upon the speed of the traverse, and is varied by altering the arrangement of change-wheels. To cut a spiral, a cutting instrument worked by the overhead apparatus is held in the rest and the proper change-wheels inserted. The gut-belt is slipped off the mandrel, and the traversing effected by turning the latter by hand. The shape of the spiral is determined by the change-wheels used and the shape of the drill.

A step-shaped spiral is made by first cutting a spiral to a certain depth with a wide drill, then inserting a narrower drill, and cutting a little deeper, and repeating the process with a still narrower drill if necessary.

Hollow spirals are cut by first turning a tube of wood, plugging it with a wood cylinder to enable it to stand the cut, and then cutting a spiral right through it with a revolving drill.

Spirals above a certain degree of coarseness cannot always be cut with this apparatus. They are cut with the spiral chuck, which consists of a piece of metal screwed on to the mandrel, and screwed to receive the ordinary chucks. It carries an index-plate and catch, also a cog-wheel, so that it can be connected with the change-wheels.

The Geometric Chuck.—The geometric chuck is the most beautiful and elaborate instrument which the ornamental turner can use. There are two kinds, the simple and compound. The simple geometric chuck is an arrangement of cog-wheels and slides for producing two rotary movements in parallel planes. The chuck screws on to the end of the mandrel, and an ordinary chuck containing the wood is screwed to its right-hand end. The cutting is done by a pointed tool held in the slide-rest. Before the chuck is used, the necessary adjustments are made by altering the slides. The lathe is then set in motion, the point of the tool brought into contact with the wood, and no farther attention is required. The tool cuts out the pattern in a continuous curved line, and eventually returns to the point from which it started. The motion of the wood resembles the motion of a planet, since it revolves on its own axis, and at the same time revolves about another centre.

The compound geometric chuck has an arrangement for producing three rotary movements in parallel planes. The variety of patterns which can be cut with this instrument is practically endless.

Many patterns are improved by being cut with beaded or curved tools. The patterns may be made very effective by veneering the face of the wood to be turned with a thin plate of wood which contrasts well with it, and then allowing the tool to cut through the veneer, thus exposing the wood beneath.

SECTION XI.—CABINET-MAKING

BY

R. W. COLE

Section XI.—CABINET-MAKING

CHAPTER I

NOTES ON TRAINING, TIMBER, SETTING-OUT, AND TOOLS

Training.—In a simple treatise it is quite impossible to convey any adequate idea of the art of cabinet-making. So much could be said that it is most difficult to know what to leave out, and however fully this subject may be enlarged upon, the broad fact that but one-half has been told must still remain. Further, a budding cabinet-maker will learn more during the first twelve months of his apprenticeship than all the text-books in the country can teach him. The old Roman motto, *Experientia docet*, is truer to-day than ever. Experience has been, and will ever be, the best teacher; but just as it is possible to start in life with better prospects upon the solid foundations laid by one's forbears, so by the aid of a few practical suggestions may a youth be helped upward on the ladder of perfection. The cabinet-maker must always strive after excellence. There is absolutely no room for men who are only half-masters of their craft; the net result of incompetence is a general levelling of the highest to the least efficient, a diminution of the rate of wages, and a disastrous lowering of the quality of work. The examples of Tudor, Elizabethan, and Queen Anne workmanship should incite the cabinet trade of to-day to patient and thoughtful work. It may be urged—and possibly truly—that these master-pieces of which we speak were not the daily product of the age which produced them. That inferior work was then produced may be admitted; but the mere fact that time has wrought its destruction should be sufficient evidence that this class of work is not such as the twentieth-century cabinet-maker should imitate.

And here one word to the journeyman of to-day. The apprentice working under your superintendence will be exactly as you make him. Men are copyists ever, and youth is the most impressionable period. See to it, then, that your work be such as the novice treading in your footsteps may safely follow. And let the apprentice benefit by his master's experience, commencing where the latter leaves off, and thus raising the handicraft to a higher level of excellence. The only true way to success is that the heart be in the work; toiling not merely for the "standard wage", nor creating a piece of work only to "sell", but to last.

Just as to-morrow is the child of to-day, so is the journeyman the fulfilment of the apprenticeship. The groundwork of early days is the foundation upon which the after-work stands, and if the first be faulty then is there but inefficiency hereafter. One word as to the influence of trades-unionism upon the cabinet trade—it has its strong and weak points. On the one hand it demands, and rightly, from the master a standard rate of wage, which is beneficial insomuch that it puts all union shops on the same level, and prevents that "cutting" policy which is alike disastrous to good work and sound finance. On the other hand it gives no guarantee of efficiency in the worker; good and bad are linked in one union, with the result that the least efficient are often out of work and maintained at the expense of their more skilled brothers. The remedy for this seems to lie here: let no man be made a member until he has passed through a satisfactory apprenticeship, and

247

proved himself to be thoroughly acquainted with his trade, and capable of honestly earning the wage demanded; then would the term "union man" be understood to mean skill and efficiency, and be as proud a possession of the man earning it as a degree to a college graduate.

Possibly it may be thought that the preceding lines have savoured too much of the ethics of labour—of work in its highest and ideal form—rather than of the practical teaching of a competing age. But there is a danger that in the mad rush for cheap and badly-manufactured furniture the true constructive art may be lost, and a race of men produced wedded to one job, year in year out, and turning out work bearing neither the stamp of individuality nor the spirit of good workmanship.

Timber.—It is not necessary to deal at any length with this subject, as it has been fully treated in Section II. The great point to be kept in view is that the wood shall be absolutely dry; if not, then the finest work will be thrown away by reason of shrunk panels, open mitres, &c.

The cabinet-maker may have to deal with log timber or sawn boards, in either case "wet". Two methods of drying may be adopted—natural or artificial. The gradual extraction of moisture by nature's action appears the most efficient, but many are not content to wait two or three years for a log to get into condition, so that nature's work is often superseded by artificial methods of drying, viz.: (1) Steam and hot air; (2) Hot-water pipes; and (3) Hot air. Unfortunately these methods do not fully realize in practice the desired result. The nearest approach to perfection is obtained by the third method from such a heater as the "Magee"; this produces most satisfactory results, is simplicity itself, and should dry soft woods satisfactorily in about ten days at a temperature of 150° F. The temperature, however, can be increased or reduced at will. A more satisfactory way would be to heat the timber-room by this means to an even temperature of 70° F., letting the timber always remain in this atmosphere whether dry or not. The same heater would be used for warming the shops.

The Magee system is a process of drying timber by means of continuously-changed hot air passing, under natural draught, through the stacks of timber in the drying-shed. It puts to practical use the natural law that hot air will take up more moisture than cold air. Even hot air, however, cannot take up an unlimited quantity of water-vapour, and a constant change of air is necessary, so that as one volume of air approaches saturation-point it may be replaced by another. Ventilation, therefore, is an essential part of the process. The principal features of the system will be understood by reference to fig. 1022, which shows a timber-kiln (40 feet × 17 feet) on one floor, with an excavated cellar for the heater and hot-air pipes. The stove consists of a wrought-iron furnace lined with fire-clay, and placed within a larger outer iron covering; into the air-space thus formed the cold air enters, and is there heated by contact with the furnace; from this the hot air passes along the various ducts leading from the dome to the registers in the room; from these it rises, passing through the stacks of timber to the roof, then descends and escapes through the exits provided.

The room shown has an air-space of about 11,000 feet; the eight air-registers, working under normal conditions, would entirely change the air in the room every thirteen minutes.

The best method of firing these stoves is with anthracite coal, as it has greater heating power and lasts much longer than other coal; if this is not available, then coke should be used. The stove is of the slow-combustion type, and will maintain a uniform temperature through the night.

Under this process soft woods should be seasoned in three weeks at a temperature of 80°, but hard woods should be given from two to three months according to the thickness of the timber and its density. It is not advisable to raise the temperature above 120°, as higher temperatures are injurious to many kinds of timber.

But whether timber is dried naturally or artificially, care should be taken in the stacking of it. Let it be stacked on joists resting on bricks, so that there is a clear air-space beneath. If the timber is in the open air, the ground should be covered with cinders; if in a covered shed, the same, or, better still, a concrete floor.

Should a variety of thicknesses be required from one log, the heart-plank is usually used for table-legs, say 5 inches thick; other boards on each side of this are cut to the desired thicknesses (fig. 1023). When skidding timber, which should be done immediately

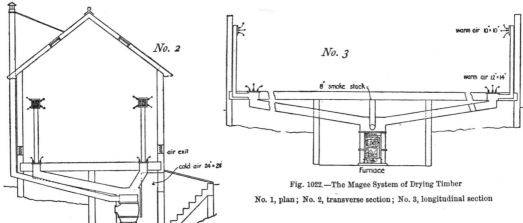

Fig. 1022.—The Magee System of Drying Timber

No. 1, plan; No. 2, transverse section; No. 3, longitudinal section

after it is sawn, let the thicker planks be placed at the bottom, working up to the thinnest (fig. 1024). Do not be afraid of using too many skids; let them be $\frac{3}{4}$ inch to 1 inch thick, to allow a good current of air between; commence at either end, and skid (say) every 2 feet 6 inches along the plank. Only by this means will warping be prevented. If boards are "steered" on end, care should be taken that they are in vertical planes, and do not touch each other. To prevent splitting, it is a good plan to nail a strip of wood on the ends of the boards, or to paint the ends.

When dry, the various thicknesses are generally stacked by themselves. This method has the advantage of saving much handling; on the other hand, it will be found better to construct a piece of work entirely from one log, for only by this means can

Fig. 1023.—Method of Cutting Log with thick Heart-plank

uniformity of colour, texture, and figure be obtained, thus saving a lot of the polisher's time in matching up the colours. This remark will apply more particularly to mahogany, in which such wide extremes are found.

In cutting out the job, study as far as possible the run of the grain in the board, in order to obtain the best results from whatever figure there may be, and also to avoid a curl or short-grain piece coming at a tenon. Also, when cutting a sweep-piece the curve should follow the grain, gaining the greatest amount of strength thereby, instead of "cross-grain", which produces in a chair-leg a decided tendency to snap off, or in a moulding requires a great deal of cleaning up. Also take care that the grain in corresponding stiles and panels runs the same way, that is, as a rule, in the direction of the longest dimension of the wood.

Fig. 1024.—Skidding Timber by Thicknesses

Setting-out.—Where a draughtsman is not employed for this purpose, the usual method of setting out a job is to make a full-size detail from the scale-drawing supplied or other information. This is done most conveniently upon 36-inch lining-paper strained upon a board, say 7 feet × 4 feet. This size will be found to be large enough for most jobs, which need only be drawn in the majority of cases to the centre line, thus showing half the width of the job, the other half being a repeat. The thickness-sections, for the sake of clearness, may be put in with blue or red pencil. Having accomplished this, the next proceeding will be to take off the drawing the various sizes of the several pieces of wood, allowing sufficient margin for finishing to the net sizes, and for the length of tenons, &c. Many of the small pieces can be obtained from the "scrap"-room, where all short ends, strips, &c., are stored in their respective classes, thus saving the cutting of a large board for the purpose of an odd rail or so, which might render it useless by reason of a corner having been cut away.

Tools.—The trade of to-day is so much the product of machine labour, that in a fully-equipped shop, where furniture is made to "stock" designs, the manual work is little more than that of fitting together the various parts. It is, however, still necessary that the craftsman should be fully acquainted with the use of the tools usually associated with the cabinet-maker's bench. The following list includes all those commonly required, but special tools may be necessary in certain cases:—

1 Folding Rule, 2 or 3 feet.	1 Bow Saw, 18 inches.	6 Hand Screws.
2 Hammers (1 Bench and 1 Framing).	1 set of Firmer Chisels, $\frac{1}{16}$ to $1\frac{1}{2}$ inch.	2 Cork Rubbers (one for mouldings).
1 Mallet.	1 ,, Mortise Chisels, $\frac{1}{8}$ to $\frac{3}{4}$ inch.	1 Scraper.
1 pair of Pincers.	1 ,, Gouges, $\frac{1}{4}$ to 1 inch.	2 Rasps, 6 and 10 inches.
3 Screwdrivers, 4, 8, and 15 inches.	2 Spoke-shaves.	2 Wood Files, 6 and 10 inches.
3 Bradauls.	1 Trying Plane.	2 Saw Files.
3 Gimlets.	1 Jack Plane.	1 Square (iron), 6 inches.
1 Brace and Bits, $\frac{3}{16}$ to $1\frac{1}{2}$ inch.	1 Smoothing Plane (wood).	1 ,, (wood), 24 inches.
1 Marking Gauge.	1 ,, (iron).	1 Bevel.
1 Cutting ,,	1 Toothing Plane.	1 Nail-punch.
1 Mortise ,,	1 Iron Rebate Plane.	1 pair of Compasses.
1 Dovetail Saw, 8 inches.	1 Wood ,,	1 Bench Holdfast.
1 Tenon ,, 14 ,,	1 Oil Stone and Can.	1 Bench Brush.
1 Hand ,, 24 ,,	1 Marker.	

CHAPTER II

JOINTS, CORNICES, AND HINGES

1. JOINTS

Edge-joints.—What may be termed "edge-joints" are a necessity in cabinet-making, because timber is not always obtainable wide enough for the counter-top or panel desired; and if it were so, the cost would prohibit its general use; but more because a jointed top or panel will stand much better than a single piece, and this is the chief thing to be aimed at. There is a tendency in some quarters to avoid jointing, but the policy is an unsound one. Again, in the case of Dantzig oak panelling, a much better effect can be obtained by

a jointed panel—throwing all the figure to the centre line—than by a single unjointed board. The chief objection to jointing seems to lie in the idea that sooner or later the joint will give; it may, just as anything is likely to happen in badly-constructed work, but given thoroughly dry and seasoned timber, a sound method of jointing, and a good workman to do it, nothing need be feared. The necessity for jointing will, of course, be governed by the width of

Fig. 1025.—Glued Edge-joint

the timber employed. It may, however, be taken as a general rule that nothing wider than 13 or 14 inches should be used in a single piece, except in the case of counter-tops, which often run 3 feet 6 inches to 4 feet wide, and would only have one joint.

There are several methods of jointing which we will now consider in detail:—(1) Glue joint; (2) Glue-and-dowel; (3) Tongue-and-groove (or rebate); and (4) Double groove and loose tongue.

1. *Glue Joint* (fig. 1025).—This is perhaps the commonest of cabinet joints for such work as bears no weight,—that is, perpendicular work, as carcass ends. The method of making the joint is briefly thus:—The two boards are shot with a trying or jointing plane until the surface edges are absolutely true; one piece is placed in the bench-cramp, the other being held so that the two edges are together; run thin glue along the joint, then work the loose board backward and forward along its fellow until the superfluous glue

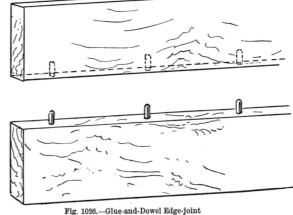

Fig. 1026.—Glue-and-Dowel Edge-joint

is extracted; the joint should now be allowed to set. If the work has been well done the wood is much more likely to break at some other point than the joint. Complete success depends upon two factors—true jointing with the plane, and good glue. There are so many good makes of the latter that there should be no difficulty whatever in obtaining it. Remember that the best glue is always the cheapest, for two reasons—its adhesive qualities and capacity for absorption of water. Good glue should take up its own weight of water, *i.e.* 1 lb. of glue in the cake should produce 2 lbs. weight in liquid form. The joint to be glued should be thoroughly warmed, as this makes the glue much more adhesive than if applied to a cold surface.

2. *Glue-and-Dowel Joint* (fig. 1026).—This method consists of jointing as in No. 1, with the addition of a series of dowels placed along the joint, the object being to ensure greater strength for such purposes as a counter-top. The dowels may be $\frac{3}{8}$ inch or $\frac{1}{2}$ inch in diameter, according to the thickness of the timber to be jointed. They should be placed (say) 12 inches apart and bored in 1 inch deep, the end of the dowel glued and knocked in with a framing hammer, then sawn off to the depth of the corresponding hole, and the

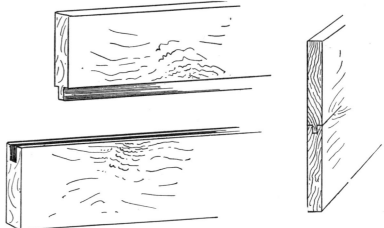

Fig. 1027.—Tongue-and-Groove Joint

ends of the dowels rounded over; glue both edges of the joint, the dowels, and dowel-holes, knock down, and cramp up. The superfluous glue will thus be squeezed out, and when the glue has set, the boards can be levelled off.

3. *Tongue-and-Groove Joint* (fig. 1027).—This joint possesses advantages not found in the preceding ones, viz. a greater strength, and should the joint "give", the presence of the tongue prevents light from showing through. With a pair of match-planes make a groove on one piece one-third the width of the timber used, by half an inch deep, and make a corresponding tongue on the other piece. When this has been done, fit the two together, seeing that the tongue will move freely along the groove, then glue and rub together as in No. 1, and cramp up.

4. *Double Groove and Loose Tongue* (fig. 1028).—The main idea in this method seems to be that when jointing two soft-woods together a hard-wood tongue (which should be

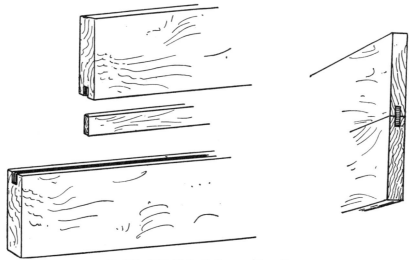

Fig. 1028.—Joint with Double Groove and Loose Tongue

cut across the grain) may be inserted, rendering the joint less liable to snap than if a tongue were cut on the soft-wood itself and lengthways with the grain. Proceed as in No. 3, only making two grooves, each the same width and depth; glue the joint and loose tongue; rub, and cramp up.

Jointing at Angles, or Framing Joints.—We have previously spoken of straight jointing for panels, carcass ends, &c., but the methods described are not suitable for the joints of pieces meeting at an angle, as in the framing of a door or of panelling.   Joints of this kind may be considered under four heads:—(1) Dovetailing; (2) Mortise-and-tenon; (3) Dowel; and (4) Mitre.   Two broad principles would seem to govern these, viz. that the wood employed be absolutely dry, and that the joint be true.   Any deviation from either of these fixed rules must result in failure; and the second is to a large extent dependent on the first, for however good the workmanship may be, if the wood be unseasoned shrinkage must inevitably occur, with the result that it is almost impossible to put the work right when once the job has been framed up.   Hence the necessity of re-insisting that absolutely dry timber is an essential in the cabinet trade.

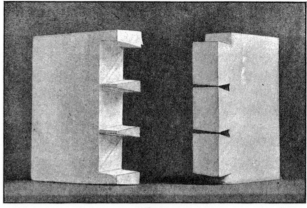

No. 1

1. *Dovetailing* (fig. 1029).—This is undoubtedly the joint *par excellence* for cabinet work; it takes three forms.   No. 1 represents the ordinary open dovetail. Each piece to be dovetailed is marked with a gauge and regulator, spacing the dovetails according to the width of wood to be jointed.   This form is used wherever the construction is hidden from view, its defect being that the ends of the dovetail are cut completely through, thus showing, if exposed, the end grain of the "keys" of the other piece.   When this is not desired the dovetail is made as No. 2. All dovetails should be cut wedge-shaped, so that when glued and hammered they will tighten up, and when smoothed down present a perfect joint.

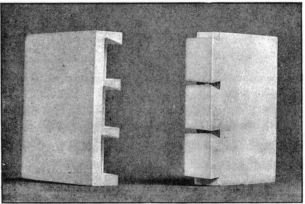

No. 2

The overlapping or concealed dovetail (No. 2) is used in drawer fronts, where it is desirable to conceal the mode of construction.   The dovetail is cut entirely through the side, but only two-thirds through the front; the joint, therefore, is visible on the end only and not on the front.   This is an absolute necessity in the case of veneering, for which purpose

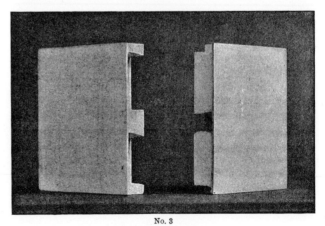

No. 3

Fig. 1029.—Dovetail-Joints

No. 1, open; No. 2, overlapping; No. 3, mitred

an absolutely flat surface must be obtained, otherwise the "keys" would show through the thin veneer and spoil the whole effect.   The jointing up and finishing is precisely the same as in No. 1.

The mitre-dovetail (No. 3) is adopted for fine work where it is undesirable to show the dovetail either on front or side, and consists of a dovetail having a mitre on each outside edge; the finished joint appears as a simple mitre without disclosing the dovetail within.

2. *Mortise-and-Tenon* (fig. 1030).—This is the most satisfactory joint for two pieces in the same plane meeting at an angle; it takes a variety of forms. The main point to be borne in mind is that the parts to form the joint be cut true; otherwise, either the tenon will be slack and the joint useless, or too tight and will split open the mortise.

The mortise should be a little longer than the tenon, and should taper inward toward its base, so that the tenon will be slightly wedged. Other methods of fixing the joint are: (1) to make the mortise large enough to admit of a wedge being driven in on each side the tenon, which effectually "keys" it; in this case the tenon is usually put in dry, that is without glue; and (2) to split open the tenon with a

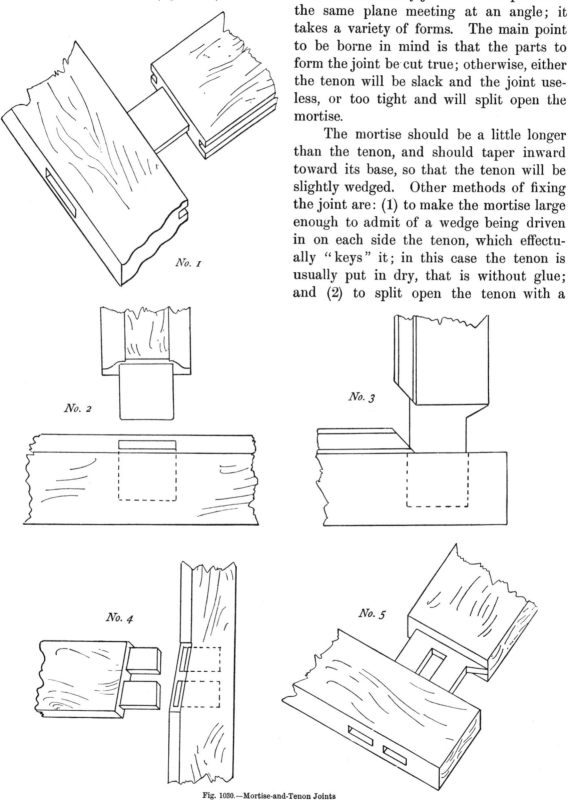

Fig. 1030.—Mortise-and-Tenon Joints

chisel, and insert a wedge in the centre and drive home. The danger of this method is that the tenon is liable to be necked off at the shoulder, while in the former case the rail may be split. If the mortise and tenon are fitted true, no wedging should be necessary.

The thickness of the tenon should be one-third that of the rail and the

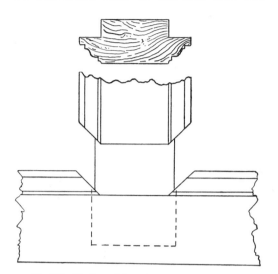

Fig. 1031.—Mortise-and-Tenon Joint with Mitred Moulds

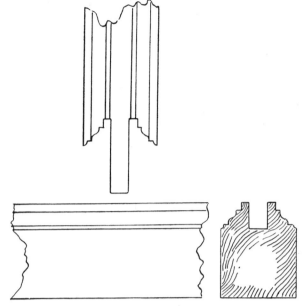

Fig. 1032.—Mortise-and-Tenon Joint with Scribed Moulds

width not more than 4 inches. If a wider rail has to be used, it would be better to make two mortises and tenons, as shown in Nos. 4 and 5.

No. 1.—Ordinary " cut-through " mortise. The tenon can be made as shown, or of the full width between the grooves, which are made on either side for the purpose of receiving the panels.

Nos. 2 and 3.—Joints for panel framing with internal mortises. These should be cut slightly deeper than the tenon, the joint being glued up and cramped.

Nos. 4 and 5.—Methods of framing wide rails by means of double-tenons,—suitable for doors where wide rails are necessary. No. 4 is usually called a gunstock joint.

In framing angles having moulds on one or both edges, the moulds may be intersected either by mitring or scribing. In the mitred joint, the moulds are cut down at an angle of 45 degrees to the mortise-hole, and the moulds adjoining the tenon are cut to fit. The only danger in this method is that, if the wood is wet, the mitre will dry in, leaving an open space impossible to deal with.

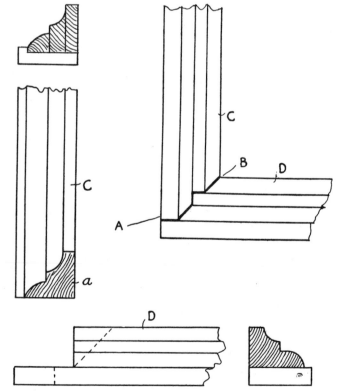

Fig. 1033.—Scribed Joint for Panel-mouldings

The process of scribing (fig. 1032) is to cut under one of the rails to the pattern of the other which it is intended to join; but this cannot so easily be done with mouldings containing many members, as it would be too costly. It, however, has the advantage that, if shrinkage occurs, the joint can be knocked up again, which would be impossible in the former case.

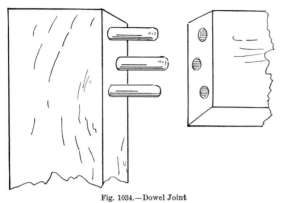

Fig. 1034.—Dowel Joint

These remarks apply to moulds worked upon the solid; loose or "planted" moulds are usually mitred, although not invariably. Fig. 1033 shows a scribed joint for panel-mouldings. The vertical moulding C is cut away at a to fit on to the horizontal moulding D. The thick line A B shows the line the scribe will make at the point of intersection.

3. *Dowel-Joint* (fig. 1034).—This method, though often adopted, as it economizes labour, is not as satisfactory as the mortise-and-tenon. The dowels, which are usually ⅜ inch in diameter, often shrink, causing the joint to "give". If the dowels are of beech and the timber dry, the joint should be satisfactory. The usual method of setting out a dowel-joint is

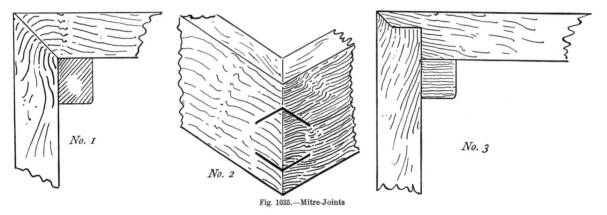

Fig. 1035.—Mitre-Joints

to cut a piece of paper the size of the rail and prick through the centres required according to the number of dowels desired. These are afterwards marked upon the timber itself. If

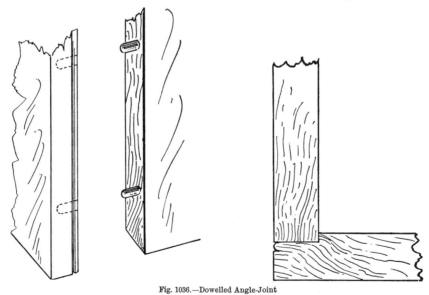

Fig. 1036.—Dowelled Angle-Joint

the wood is not more than 1 inch thick, the dowels should be set out in the centre of the rail in a straight line; if thicker wood is used, put the dowels in zigzag fashion, which is the better way where it can be managed.

4. *Mitring, &c.*—Where small sizes are used, the joint at the angle formed by two pieces not in the same plane is usually mitred. The construction of the joint is thus hidden.

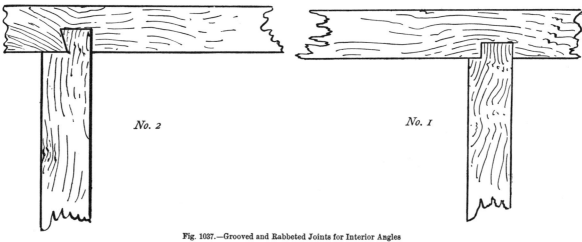

Fig. 1037.—Grooved and Rabbeted Joints for Interior Angles
No. 1, square; No. 2, dovetailed

No. 1, fig. 1035, shows an ordinary mitre at an angle of 45 degrees, such as is used in the framing of a plinth or cornice frieze; the joint is strengthened by a block inside.

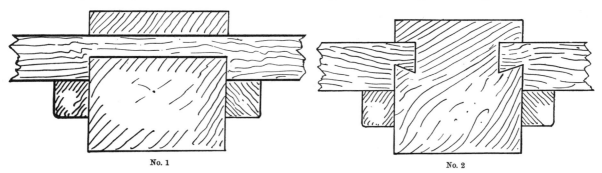

No. 2 represents the same method, with the additional safeguard of keys; this would be adopted in the case of thin wood where the mitre surface is very small, and where there is consequently a liability to break; the keys are usually put in with veneer, a saw-cut being all that is necessary for their insertion. Glue is run in and the joint levelled off.

No. 3 is a variation of No. 1.

Fig. 1036 shows an angle framed

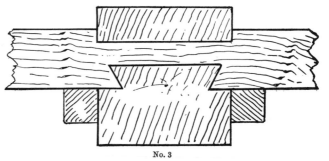

Fig. 1038.—Joints between Rails and Legs

by dowels, having on the one edge a bead, which breaks the joint; this would be used in framing a pilaster upon the end of a carcass.

Fig. 1037 shows two methods of framing an interior angle.

No. 1, fig. 1038, shows the method of framing a through rail intersected into a centre leg, not more than 3 inches square. No. 2 shows the construction if the centre leg is above that size, and is not mortised or dowelled. No. 3 is copied from an old card-table; the shouldering and dovetailing of the rail show advantages in strength over No. 1.

2. CORNICES

A cornice may be worked out of the solid piece or built up in various pieces. The latter form is usually adopted by cabinet-makers, except for small cornices. No. 1, fig. 1039, shows a built-up mould; the pieces should be glued and screwed together, blocks

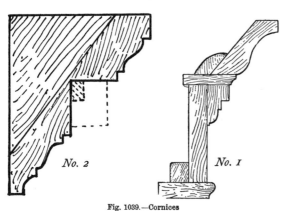

Fig. 1039.—Cornices
No. 1, Built-up; No. 2, solid hardwood faced on softwood

being put at the back to give additional strength. No. 2 shows a solid hardwood moulding faced upon softwood, the mould having a rebate for the insertion of a dentil (shown by the dotted lines), egg-and-dart, or other ornament.

Ofttimes the cabinet-maker is left to design the mouldings, in which case it is absolutely necessary that he be thoroughly conversant with the mouldings of the particular style or period in which he is working, as a Gothic mould would be out of place upon a Renaissance piece of work, and a Jacobean cornice upon a Sheraton job. If the designer is not conversant with the grammar of ornament, all kinds of incongruous mixtures are created, neither true to style nor beautiful. The same remarks apply also to carving and turnery, and as there are so many text-books of style published, there is absolutely no excuse for ignorance in this matter.

Another point upon which a word may be said is the proportioning of mouldings one to the other in the building-up of a cornice. Let it be supposed that one has to be struck

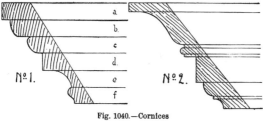

Fig. 1040.—Cornices
No. 1, With members of equal depth; No. 2, with members of varying depth

by hand. It is frequently possible to pick out a series of stock members all the same size, and to strike out a variety of cornices by ringing the changes on them. The result, however, will be a moulding as shown in No. 1, fig. 1040, where all the members, a, b, c, d, e, f, are of equal depth. This is both incorrect and inelegant; no moulding made up of a series of members should have any two in conjunction of the same depth, but the proportion should be varied after the manner shown in No. 2, the effect of which—it will be at once apparent —is much better than No. 1.

3. HINGES

In cabinet-work the methods of hanging a door, table-leaf, &c., to its corresponding part, are simple, and the formation of the joint varies but little, though in the case of hanging a door with heavy projecting moulding and cornice upon the face, special long-shouldered butts would be used. The main point in all hanging by means of hinges is to see that each hinge bears its due proportion of weight, thus avoiding strain and consequent friction and possibly breakage.

Hinges may be of cast or malleable iron, steel, brass, copper, gun-metal, or a combination of metals, such as brass with steel washers; for heavy work these washers should always be used, the wearing parts being stronger.

The earliest form of hinge seems to have been in the form of an oak pin (A, fig. 1041) shaped from the rail itself, and working in a socket cut into the cross rail above, the doors

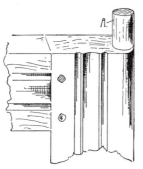

Fig. 1041.—Hanging Stile of Door opening on Pivots

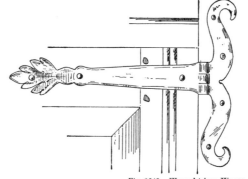

Fig. 1042.—Wrought-iron Hinges

being framed up with the job itself; the form is common in fifteenth and sixteenth century wood-work.   Later, the influence of Flemish work is apparent, and the pin-joint gives place to wrought-iron hinges placed upon the face of the door and frame with artistic effect, and attached by means of large-headed nails (fig. 1042).   During the Queen Anne and Chippendale periods, the hinges were delicately made of cast brass and fixed by screws.

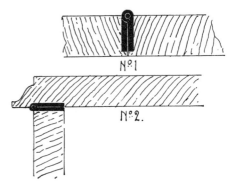

Fig. 1043.—Butt Hinges.   No. 1, For door; No. 2, for lid

The ordinary way of hanging by butts is shown in No. 1, fig. 1043; the rebate is not carried through the wood, and the knuckle projects on the front side. If this is not desired, the hinge must be fixed flush, and a bead of the same thickness as the knuckle run down to make a better finish.   When a lid is to be hinged, it would be done as in No. 2, the overhang at the back being, in the case of a small lid, sufficient to serve as a stop when the lid is open.

In hanging a table-leaf, many forms may be adopted.   No. 1, fig. 1044, shows a beaded and rebated joint, the centre of the hinge being directly under the joint.   Except for dust-proof or light-tight purposes, the rebate is not necessary.   This joint would open to 90°.   Should the leaf or door require to fold back behind the other part, the hinge should be placed as shown in No. 2, the dotted lines showing the position of the leaf when folded back.   Another form of leaf hanging is that known as a "rule joint", which is shown closed in No. 3, and open in No. 4.   This has the advantage of concealing the hinge, and making a better finish when open than

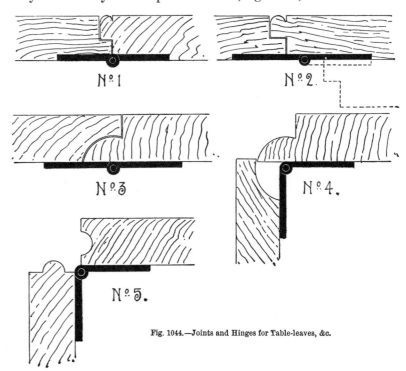

Fig. 1044.—Joints and Hinges for Table-leaves, &c.

otherwise would be the case; the joint is somewhat difficult to get true, but always repays the labour in effect.   A variation of this joint is shown in No. 5.

Carcass doors are generally hung as shown in No. 1, fig. 1045, a bead the size of the knuckle being run down to break the joint, and the hinge being rebated into the door its entire thickness.   No. 2 shows the method of hanging on to the ends of a carcass, where the full clearance of the door is desired, such as would be the case in a cupboard fitted

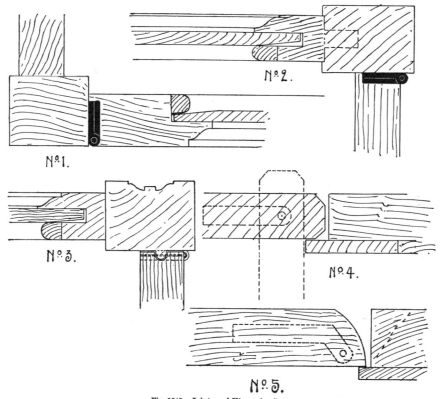

Fig. 1045.—Joints and Hinges for Doors

with sliding trays.   No. 3 shows the same method, but with air-tight bead for a cabinet or show-case.

Centre hanging, as for wardrobe doors, is shown in Nos. 4 and 5, the door being set back in a rebate, or having a pilaster planted on to hide the joint.   Sometimes this joint is made on the rule principle, but this adds to the expense.

Special hinges, such as are made for card-tables, bureaus, pianos, ·&c., while varying in shape and size to suit requirements, are fitted in exactly the same manner as the foregoing illustrations indicate.

CHAPTER III

VENEERING, POLISHING, STAINING, &c.

1. VENEERING

This process consists of laying an expensive or highly-figured wood upon a foundation of common wood.   It does not always meet with approval, the prevailing idea being that if a piece of cabinet-work is veneered it is cheap; but a moment's consideration would convince the incredulous that the finest effects are to be obtained only in this way.   A visit to the timber-yard will at once reveal logs for sawing into boards, and also logs for veneering; the latter command a higher price according to their size or the richness of the figure.   The best wood is usually to be found at the butt of the tree, though good mottle may be obtained at the junction of the trunk and limbs. In buying a log for veneering purposes, only long experience can determine its quality and worth; the external appearance is not always a true index of the internal, and it is often a matter of chance, the most unlikely log when opened up turning out to be finely-figured wood.

Cutting Veneers.—Veneers are of two kinds—" sawn " and " knife-cut ".

" Sawn."—This term is applied to all veneers that are cut by saw. The log is placed upon a travelling platform, the fine saws being set in a vertical frame and cutting the veneers simultaneously through the log. The usual number of veneers to the inch is ten, but, if desired, twelve may be obtained; the latter are, however, thin, and not so serviceable. The veneers are numbered consecutively, so that " match " veneers may easily be determined. The ends should be bound with muslin to prevent splitting. Veneers to be in proper workable order must be kept in a damp place; they are then much more pliable, and less liable to crack. The waste of timber in cutting by this method is, roughly speaking, about $\frac{3}{8}$ of an inch per inch of thickness.

" Knife-cut."—By this method there is no waste whatever. The log, having been opened up, is steamed and, while saturated with moisture, placed under the knife. This works horizontally, and takes off the thinnest shaving possible. The usual number of veneers obtained per inch of thickness is from thirty-six to forty; they are therefore almost as thin as paper, and not at all reliable for hard wear or subsequent scraping and repolishing. Knife-cut veneers should only be used on those parts of a job that are not liable to constant wear; the only advantage—and that a doubtful one—which they possess is that the veneer will " lie " more readily upon a sweep or on the flat owing to its thinness, and with a reduction in time there is a corresponding abatement in price. Apart from economic reasons, a " sawn " veneer should always be used.

Veneering.—Any wood is suitable for veneering upon, but those usually selected are of the " bay-wood " or pine orders. The foundation, having been faced up, is " toothed " by a hand plane, thus imparting a rough surface to the wood which will enable the glue to adhere more firmly. A solution of size and water used hot is next applied and allowed to dry. The heart side of a board should always be veneered upon, and the reverse side damped with water to prevent the board going round when sized. Lay the board face down until ready for veneering. The veneer may now be laid, and can be done in two ways— by hand or machine. For small works, mouldings, or sweeps, use the former method; for panels, carcass ends, &c., the latter.

Process 1.—Quickly brush over with hot glue, taking care to spread it evenly. The veneer may then be laid down, pressed by hand to remove the air, and squegeed down by means of a " cawl ", removing all blisters and superfluous glue. A weighted board should then be placed on the job until the following day. In the case of sweeps, either a steel bow-cramp contracted to the shape, or a wooden template secured by means of cramps, should be used.

Process 2.—The machine usually constructed for this purpose (fig. 1046) comprises an iron framework with perforated cast top, a series of gas-burners running at intervals of 9 inches or so the length of the machine, and over this an iron plate covered by a sheet of zinc. The gas having been turned on and the plate heated, the job to be veneered is laid on the machine, and cramps are then placed across and tightened down by means of set-screws, until the air between the foundation and the veneer is excluded, and the superfluous glue squeezed out. This may easily be ascertained by a tap on the panel, a hollow sound indicating that the veneer is not bedded. When the veneer has been laid, turn off the gas and leave the job to cool naturally, say, through the night, the cramps remaining on. After standing for three days, the work may be finished off. It will be found that some of the glue has oozed through the pores of the veneer, while a general roughness is

apparent.   Proceed with an ordinary iron scraper or iron plane to smooth down (the
latter is better if the veneer is thick enough, as the scraper may get too warm and

Fig. 1046.—Veneering Machine

soften the glue beneath), and finish with sand-paper upon a cork rubber.   The job is
then ready for the polisher.

When more than one veneer is used upon a panel, they are jointed in the following
manner:—

The butt-joint (fig. 1047) is a most effective way
of veneering a drawer-front or panel.   Take two
"match" veneers—that is, consecutive numbers—as
cut from the log, cut through each where it is desired to butt, thus making them "rights" and
"lefts", the figure falling equally from the central

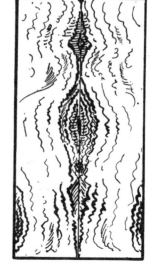

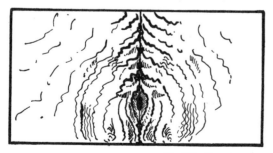

Fig. 1047.—Veneering with Butt-joint

joint.   The veneer is then laid upon the foundation, and a few needle points or tacks placed
on each side the joint, a strip of brown paper being glued upon the same to hold it in
position.   When dry, lay as before described.

Fig. 1048.—A more elaborate way of panel-veneering is to use four match veneers
quartered.   All the joints must be pasted.

Fig. 1049.—Still more elaborate is the addition of cross-banding, which is laid by hand after the centre is completed.

Fig. 1050.—The addition of a stringing is often advantageous to break the line of

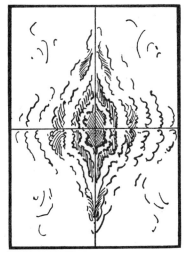

Fig. 1048.—Quartered Veneering

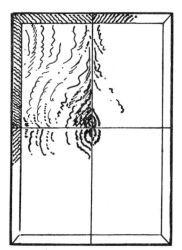

Fig. 1049.—Quartered and Cross-banded Veneering

junction and throw up the centre, a narrow band of the veneer being removed for this purpose by means of a cutting gauge.

Fig. 1051.—If there is a defect or hole in a veneer, a new piece should be inserted

Fig. 1050.—Cross-banded Veneering with Stringing

Fig. 1051.—Patch in Veneer

matching the curl or mottle of the wood, the edges of which should be cut to the shape of the curl or follow the line of the grain. If this is done, detection is almost impossible; on no account insert a square piece, as the hard lines thus produced are most objectionable.

2. FRENCH-POLISHING

This most important branch of the wood-working trade seldom gets the attention it deserves, the common idea being that there is nothing in polishing demanding skill or judgment, or even worth the trouble of knowing. No greater mistake than this could be made. Polishers have in their hands the making or marring of the finished piece of furniture from the cabinet-maker's bench. Briefly, the process of French-polishing consists in the application of various gums, lacs, &c., dissolved in spirit, in order to give to the wood a surface or polish (bright or dull as required) which not only preserves the wood, but brings out the beauty of the grain.

Workshop and Fittings.—The workshop should be a large well-ventilated building, with a north light for preference and also top lights. It should be kept heated to a given temperature, say 60° F., and be maintained at this heat night and day. Hot-water pipes around the walls, with regulating valves, will probably give the best results; steam-pipes may be used, but do not maintain such an equable temperature. A small enclosed coke-stove or gas-burner is an essential for the purpose of melting wax, obtaining hot water, &c.

The room should be free from dust, as any particles floating in the air and settling on a job in process, are bound to be worked up into it, producing a cloudy effect. There should also be a smaller room leading from the main shop for "Fumigating"; this must be air-tight, and have a pane of glass inserted in one of the upper panels of the door for observation purposes.

Trestles are required varying in height from 9 inches to 30 inches, and loose tops of different lengths and widths for placing on them. Several wooden battens covered with felt to protect a job are also necessary.

Materials.—It need hardly be said that upon the quality of the materials used in polishing depends very largely the ultimate result, good or bad. And here, as in other branches of trade, the best is always the cheapest. It will be found a mistake to lay in too much stock, as polish quickly evaporates and other materials deteriorate, but rather to buy small quantities of lacs, spirit, &c., and mix fresh as required.

Not much in the way of plant is needed to fit a polishing shop;—say, half a dozen pint (and a few larger) stoppered bottles for polish, glaze, finish, varnish, &c.; a few jars for stain, oil, fillers; and tin canisters for keeping rubbers, more valued by the polisher than any part of his kit.

How to make a Rubber.—Get a piece of clean white or gray wadding, remove the skin from it, and roll it into an egg shape, then cover the same with a thin linen rag strained tightly over the wadding, holding the ends in the palm of the hand, the two forefingers and thumb bedding themselves on the extremity of the rubber, flatten the under side or polishing surface, and you will have an oval flat of, say, 3 by 2 inches. The proper size of the rubber depends upon the polisher himself and the class of work engaged on.

If new linen or calico prints be used, they should be washed to remove all trace of lime or dressing, and be as soft and pliable as possible. A different rubber should be used for different polishes, and as they are so easy and inexpensive to make, there is no reason why work should be clouded through dirty rubbers. Cleanliness and good polishing go hand in hand. When the rubber is finished with, it should be kept in an air-tight canister. It will thus keep soft, and may be used repeatedly. Failure to do this will result in hardness, which renders it useless. We are now ready to commence work and proceed to the first stage, viz.:—

Filling-in.—This consists of coating the surface of the wood with a filler, which closes or fills up the grain, thus making it possible to get a perfectly smooth surface for polishing and also saving time and material in the after-work. Upon the efficiency of the filling-in depends the result of the finished job. There are many good fillers on the market, any one of which might be equally well adopted, but it is much better that the polisher should make his own polishes, &c., and many men prefer to do so. Consequently no two polishers use exactly the same formula, but work upon receipts best adapted to their own particular style. Before filling-in, the work should be as finely papered down as possible. Too much stress cannot be laid on this point, for if well done at first much after-labour will be saved. The filler can then be put on with a flannel, and rubbed into the grain of the wood until the pores are filled up, then wipe all off and paper down. This will be found necessary, because the filler will have raised the grain. When dry, the work will be ready for the next process, bodying-up.

The following fillers will be found useful. The exact proportions can be ascertained when mixing, remembering that the filler must just be of the consistency to work freely.

Fillers.—(1) *Spirit varnish* laid on with a brush; this forms a good quick filler. Two coats should be given.

(2) *Size.*—Ordinary glue size may be used as a filler in the case of hard-grained wood, and will answer the purpose.

(3) *Whiting and Linseed-oil.*—Mix these together into a paste and apply with a flannel. This is a filler generally adopted.

(4) *Whiting and Russian Tallow.*—Mix to a paste and apply as before.

The disadvantage in Nos. 3 and 4 is that there is a great liability to get the job greasy, which will afterwards work its way through the polish, giving the surface a cobweb effect which is known as "sweating".

(5) *Plaster of Paris and Water.*—Mix as required, and apply to the job, and rub off as quickly as possible. This filler is undoubtedly the cleanest and most effectual that can be used, and entirely obviates "sweating".

(6) *Whiting and Turpentine.*—Mix into a paste, and apply as before. This is preferred by many to No. 5.

Thus far these fillers are in the white, and suitable only for such woods as ash, satin-wood, birch, &c. In the case of dark-coloured woods the filler should be tinted as nearly as possible to the colour of the wood. Thus, for mahogany it should be tinted with rose-pink or venetian red; ebonized work, lamp-black; oak, walnut woods, &c., chromes, ochres, and umbers according to the tone required.

Bodying-up.—We now come to the second stage of polishing. The wood having been again papered down with fine old glass paper, take a rubber, previously described, and sprinkle a little polish on to it from the stock bottle; then cover over with a rag, holding the ends tightly in the palm of the hand, and tap the rubber against the palm of the other hand, which will cause the polish to distribute itself over the whole rubber; put a spot of linseed-oil on with the finger, and the rubber is ready for work. Commence very lightly at one corner of the work, if it be a panel or carcass end, and by a series of motions forming interlacing curves, gradually work over the entire surface, never lifting the rubber until at the edge of the job. Care must be taken not to have the rubber too full of polish, or to press on the work too hard, in which case the polish will ooze out of the rubber and leave nasty ridges on the job; the idea is how best to cover the entire work evenly. Having done this, let the job stand as long as possible—a few days will do no harm,—the shellac will then have sunk into the wood, the spirit evaporating. This will present a dull appearance, and feel rough to the touch. We then proceed to paper down again, in fact too much stress cannot be placed upon the value of judicious sand-papering. After this the operation is repeated until a good body of polish is obtained on the work. Be very sparing of using oil; though this eases the rubber, it ruins the job ultimately. After another papering or pumice-stoning down we can pass to the final stage, spiriting-off. It may be asked, how many times is it necessary to go over the work? This very much depends on the wood worked upon. It will be anything from three to six times, the object being to obtain a body, hard and that will not sink. Much of the modern work is completely ruined to-day because it is "rushed". Time is not allowed between the rubbers, consequently no proper foundation is obtained, and in six months' time the job requires redoing. The method described above will apply equally to either light or dark woods, the difference being in the polish used rather than the method.

Spiriting-off.—This process may be called the most difficult portion of French-polishing, and when once proficient in this a man may be said to know his trade. The process is similar to bodying-up, with this exception, that toward the last "spirits" only are used on the rubber. This has the effect of polishing the "lac" put on during bodying-up, and giving to the work a fine, hard, bright surface; the oil previously worked in is spirited out.

Commence by using, say, two parts of polish to one of spirit, then equal parts, afterwards two of spirit to one of polish, and thus gradually reducing the polish to nil, and using only pure spirit. The rubber and motions are as previously described. A clean rubber should be used when pure spirit only is used, and a series of straight motions taken instead of the circular ones, running the same direction as the grain of the wood.

Small mouldings, angles, awkward corners, &c., which would be very difficult to spirit-off in the ordinary way, may be done by "glazing". Applied with a rubber and worked straight along the moulds, this glaze quickly dries, and has the same appearance as if spirited-off. It is, however, softer, and will not stand wear. Much of this work could be obviated if the polisher were given the job in pieces; for instance, mouldings mitred around panels should be polished in long lengths, and cut and fitted afterwards, thus avoiding nasty corners. Turned work is better polished in the lathe, before being framed up. Panels should be polished before framing up, or if beaded in, left loose for that purpose.

Receipts for French Polish.—There is absolutely no difficulty in mixing polishes, and every man should be able to do so, the process simply consisting in dissolving shellac in methylated spirit. This latter should be bought at 60 over-proof, stored in a cool place, and tightly sealed, as it soon evaporates.

Shellac is orange in colour; the lighter the colour the purer the quality. It is in small flakes, and requires crushing before dissolving in the spirits. This would be used for ordinary polish. If, however, a clear or white polish is desired, then bleached shellac is used. This is in lumps, and must be crushed before using. This lac must be kept in water. Colouring pigments can be added to any polish to intensify it as desired, such as Bismarck or Vandyke brown. These polishes should be mixed cold—the shellac will take a little longer to dissolve, but the operation is much safer,—then strain through muslin, and put in stoppered bottles.

Brown Polish.—(1) 1 pint methylated spirit, 4 ozs. orange shellac; or (2) 1 pint methylated spirit, 5 ozs. orange shellac, $\frac{1}{2}$ oz. sandarac; or (3) 1 pint methylated spirit, 4 ozs. orange shellac, $\frac{1}{2}$ oz. sandarac, $\frac{3}{4}$ oz. benzoin

White Polish.—1 pint methylated spirit, 3 ozs. bleached shellac, 1 oz. gum benzoin.

Black Polish.—Either Nos. 1, 2, or 3, adding drop-black or an aniline dye.

Glaze.—1 pint methylated spirit, 6 ozs. benzoin. $\frac{1}{2}$ oz. of sandarac can be added for hardening purposes.

Furniture Revivers.—Under this head come those preparations which are used to restore furniture which has already been polished, but has through neglect or other cause become cloudy. The first thing to be done in a case of this kind is to thoroughly wash the woodwork with a flannel soaped with curd soap and warm water; by this means all dirt and grease will be removed. After wiping down with a soft dry duster, apply one or other of the following revivers, and polish off with another clean duster. Much of the old polish will thus be brought back.

Reviver No. 1.—Take equal parts of methylated spirit, linseed-oil, and malt vinegar. Mix well and shake before using.

Reviver No. 2.—Turpentine, 1 quart; bees'-wax, $\frac{3}{4}$ lb.; curd soap, 2 oz.; water, 1 quart. Dissolve the bees'-wax in the turpentine by moderate heat; shred the curd soap in the water and boil; then while both are hot mix together. This will set in a light paste, and prove an excellent polisher.

Repairs.—When a bruise has to be made good upon a job the best plan to adopt is as follows:—Raise the bruise by means of a hot iron placed upon a damp cloth. This, unless the wood is broken, will lift it to its original level, it may then be sand-papered off and polished.

Bleaching.—It sometimes happens that some parts of the wood are darker than the rest, in which event it is most important that the darker parts be reduced to the lighter. This result is produced by bleaching. Dissolve 1 oz. of oxalic acid in half a pint of water, and apply with a rag; when dry, paper down, and if the density is not sufficiently reduced, repeat the operation until the desired result is obtained.

Sweating-out.—When too much oil has been used on the job, the surface presents a cobweb appearance which gradually increases and eats the polish away. When first detected, it may be removed with warm water, soap, and flannel; but when of long standing, nothing can be done to remove it except repolishing.

3. FUMIGATING

This is the process of treating oak with ammonia, darkening it by this means to any required shade. This result can be achieved in two ways.

(1st) Natural fumigation, that is, exposing the oak work in a sealed chamber to the fumes of ammonia until the required density is obtained.

(2nd) By applying liquid ammonia to the job itself.

The ammonia used should be a solution of ammonia gas in water, and should have a specific gravity of ·880. This must, on account of its volatile nature, be kept in a well-stoppered bottle.

Process 1.—To fumigate by this means a separate chamber is required. This may be an ordinary room or a fuming-cabinet built in the corner of the polishing shop. In either case it must be air-tight, and the door opening into it should have a square of glass for observation purposes. When the oak work has been placed within it, take, say, 1 pint of ammonia and fill about a dozen saucers placed upon the floor. The door must then be closed, and sealed up by means of brown paper pasted round the joints. The process of fuming then begins, and can be watched through the glass until the desired shade is obtained. The smaller the chamber the quicker will the work be done; the time may vary from six to twelve hours according to the strength of the ammoniated atmosphere. Practice alone will determine the time for opening the chamber. This is the only reliable and safe way of fumigating; in fact all other processes are but imitations of it, and the product of "cheapness and rush".

The advantages of this process are: (1) that as no liquid touches the job the grain is not raised, consequently sand-papering is avoided; (2) the ammonia fumes penetrate deeper into the wood than by outward application; (3) the exact density can be more easily determined.

The disadvantages are: (1) This process requires a separate room for the purpose; (2) it takes much more time than is required by the direct application of ammonia.

In connection with natural fuming it will be noticed that some parts of the job may not "take" at all. This often arises from the fact that various oaks have been used in its construction. Thus "Dantzic" will be susceptible to the fumes, while "American" will not. Those parts which have not "taken" must then be treated by Process 2, and care must be exercised that the resultant colour may be the same. Let the ammonia for this purpose be very weak. Let it dry before applying another coat (if necessary), as it is much easier to intensify than to bleach, and nothing looks worse than a patchy job.

Process 2.—This consists in the application of liquid ammonia (·880 spec. grav.) direct on to the work. It is usually applied with a sponge or rag. Water may be added to weaken the solution if only a light tint is desired. The wood immediately darkens upon the surface, but allowances should be made for its drying lighter. The objection to this process is that it raises the grain, which entails sand-papering down, while process No. 1

does not. This necessarily takes away much of the sharpness of the mouldings, the fillets suffering most of all. In this case it will be found that the work does not take the dye evenly, and the same shading or toning to a colour will be found necessary to produce a good result.

In either process the job should be in the white, that is, without brass or copper work or silvered plates, as these are liable to be affected by the ammonia fumes.

Finishing.—The work, having been fumed by either of the foregoing processes, is now ready for finishing, and the usual way is either of the following:—(1) Egg-shell finish; (2) Wax finish.

(1) Apply a thin rubber of ordinary polish to the job, and dull down with powdered pumice-stone and a stiff brush. This will give a dull shine without in any way filling the grain of the wood.

(2) Dissolve pure bees'-wax in turpentine, and apply with a rag, rubbing well in, and obtaining a polish by "elbow grease". This is a more tedious process than the former, but much more satisfactory, as this process can be carried on after the job has left the polisher's hands and the polish will constantly improve.

Mahogany is the only other wood that will "fume". It assumes a purple tint, and should be treated in the same manner as oak.

4. WAX-POLISHING

This method of producing a polish was undoubtedly the earliest adopted by cabinet-makers, and is best suited to the finishing of English oak, elm, chestnut, or yew tree. The advantage appears to consist in the fact that the process is never complete, and, like Tennyson's "Brook", may go on for ever. Much of the beauty of a piece of sixteenth-century carved oak is due to the polishing,—the result of years of rubbing.

In wax-polishing two ingredients only are necessary, bees'-wax and turpentine. The wax should be melted, and sufficient turpentine added to form an easy workable paste; do not heat the turpentine or pour it into the melted wax while the latter is still on the fire, as it is highly inflammable. As all the turpentine must evaporate before the polishing is complete—leaving the wax to act as both filler and polisher,—no more should be added at the commencement than necessary, otherwise the work will be prolonged. If the stock sets hard it can be softened again by warming, but it is better to mix it in small quantities as required. The safest method of warming or melting all ingredients in the polish-shop is by steam, using a kettle or double pan, such as the cabinet-makers use for glue. This point is one not lost sight of by insurance companies.

In applying the wax-polish no skill is required, but "elbow-grease" and patience are absolutely necessary.

We will suppose that we are polishing an oak dado, which has been previously fumed or stained. If the latter, we shall rub down with sand-paper; if the former, this will be unnecessary. By means of a flannel boss we apply the wax-polish, rubbing the panels in circular motion till every part receives an equal amount. This first application will simply act as a "filler", and not produce any polish. The work may now with advantage be laid aside until the next day, when the process may be repeated. Let "a little and often" be the motto,—*a little*, in order that no clagging of wax occurs in the corners and mouldings, all the wax being rubbed in until an even bright surface is obtained, free from all tackiness or finger marking; and *often*, so that each thin coat may have a chance to sink into the grain and by the evaporation of the turpentine harden. Remember that the polish is produced not by the amount of wax used but by "elbow-grease".

If preferred, a piece of felt glued on to a wooden block may be used; a stiff flat bristle brush is often used for polishing a carved panel or turned work.

Thus far we have spoken of wax-polishing as applied to oak, and it is questionable whether it can be applied with equal success to other woods; stained ash is perhaps the next best wood to oak for this method of polishing.

Floors are often treated in this way, including parquet surrounds, plain stained surrounds, or entire floors. Hard-wood floors are usually polished without previous staining, as each polishing darkens the floor until a rich tone results. The method is as previously described, except that for floors a box-polisher is used. This is a deal box (say) 12 × 8 × 6 inches, weighted inside with iron or lead to 14 lbs.; attached to this is a handle 6 feet long, working on a swivel, and thus allowing a sweep of 6 feet or so in each direction, in other words a clear swing of 12 feet or more. Upon the bottom of this box tack a piece of clean felt and proceed to polish.

The wax must previously have been rubbed on the floor with a flannel, and the first part of the polishing done with a weighted brush having a surface of 12 × 8 inches, and fitted with a swinging handle. This will evenly spread the wax and take up all superfluous quantities; it will also produce a certain amount of polish which can afterwards be brought up to a great brilliancy by the finishing felt polisher. This method would also be used in preparing the floor of a ball-room, which might afterwards be kept in condition by the sprinkling and rubbing-in of French chalk.

5. OIL-POLISHING

If wax-polishing was the original method of treating oak, it may be said with equal truth that oil-polishing was the method of finishing mahogany in the days when French-polishing was unknown; in fact, it is questionable whether any of the seventeenth- and eighteenth-century work was dealt with in any other manner. Chippendale, Sheraton, and their contemporaries certainly adopted it as best suited to their work, and the untouched jobs handed down prove their decision to have been right.

The great objection to oil-polishing is the length of time required to produce a good result; in fact, the longer you go on, the better it is. This fact has in these days of speed completely put oil-polishing in the background; the manufacturer wants a speedy return for his capital, and the public require their furniture the day after they give the order, so that it is impossible to have a job in the polisher's hands a month, and speedier methods have consequently been adopted.

It is unquestioned that oil-polishing will bring up the figure of mahogany and enrich its colour better than any other method, and if time permits, it is, for large work (such as panelling, dadoes, doors, screens, counter tops, &c.), the very best way of polishing.

The application consists in simply producing a polish upon the wood with raw linseed-oil, this being continually rubbed in with a flannel or felt pad. Let the operation be repeated day by day until a polish results. The process is, like wax-polishing, extremely tedious and laborious. Oil-polish can always be revived years afterwards by the same process, and a little judicious rubbing will keep the work constantly up to the mark.

6. STAINING AND VARNISHING

The rage for effect at low cost has necessitated the staining of white woods to imitate the more expensive ones, and the bulk of the so-called walnut or dark mahogany fittings are but the product of the polisher who, with dexterous hand, produces the required deception. The woods commonly used for stained work are canary wood, yellow pine, and deal.

Stains should be placed on the wood direct before any size or filling has been applied. They may be applied in warm or cold water, diluted to their proper strength. A sponge is the best medium, and care should be taken that the stain floods the wood equally. When dry, the work should be sand-papered carefully—as the wet stain raises the grain—and a smooth surface obtained, then proceed with the finishing off as previously described. Aniline dyes are much used, and can be obtained in any shade in addition to the following. Let the stain be weak; it is easier to apply a second coat than lighten the first.

Walnut.—(1) Vandyke brown, $\frac{1}{2}$ lb.; ammonia ·880, 1 pint; water, 1 quart: (2) bichromate of potash, 4 ozs.; water, 1 quart.

Mahogany.—(1) Bismarck brown, 2 ozs.; water, 1 quart: (2) logwood, $\frac{3}{4}$ lb.; water, 1 quart.

Black.—Logwood, $\frac{1}{2}$ lb.; sulphate of iron, $\frac{1}{4}$ lb.; water, 1 quart.

Green.—Sulphate of copper, 2 ozs.; chrome yellow, 4 ozs.; water, 1 quart.

Apply the stain to the wood with a sponge or rag, rubbing over the work until an even surface is obtained. Allow the stain to dry (which will raise the grain), then paper down, and proceed to finish by varnishing. This may be done in either oil or spirit, but the process is the same, except that for oil varnish a bristle brush may be used, while for spirit a camel-hair brush is desirable. After the first coat by either method, the work should be rubbed down before a second or finishing coat is applied. If an extra fine surface is required, paper down again after the second coat, and apply a third. Oil varnish would be used for such work as would be exposed to the weather, spirit varnish for indoor or protected woodwork.

The following are a few receipts for varnishes:—

Oak Varnish.—3 ozs. resin, 1 pint turps, and 4 ozs. sandarac.

Copal Varnish.—2 lbs. Sierra Leone copal, 1 lb. boiled linseed-oil, and $3\frac{1}{2}$ pints turpentine.

Spirit Varnish.—1 lb. orange shellac, 6 ozs. sandarac, 2 ozs. hard resin, and 2 qts. meth. spirit.

Clear Spirit Varnish.—8 ozs. sandarac, 1 qt. meth. spirit, $\frac{1}{8}$ pint turpentine; this should stand and be strained through muslin to take out all sediment.

Spirit Varnish.—$\frac{1}{2}$ lb. orange shellac, 1 oz. resin, 1 oz. sandarac, and 1 pint meth. spirit; this makes a hard, quick-setting varnish.

CHAPTER IV

UPHOLSTERY

Under the term "upholstery" are included (1) the Stuffing and covering of seats of all kinds; (2) Mattress making; (3) Floor-coverings; (4) Blinds; and (5) Draperies.

In this chapter we shall confine ourselves to the first of these. Floor-coverings will be briefly considered in a later chapter. The other parts of the subject do not lie within the scope of this work.

The tools required are comparatively few and inexpensive, viz.:—

2 Hammers (1 ordinary and 1 cabriole).	3 Stitching Needles (6, 9, and 12 ins.).	2 Gimlets.
Web Pincers.	1 Circular Needle.	2 Sprig Bits.
Web Strainer.	2 Packing Needles (4 and 6 inches).	3-feet Folding Rule.
2 Screw-drivers (say 6 and 9 inches).	Regulator.	33-feet Tape Measure.
Ripping Chisel.	Steel Skewers.	1 pair of Large Scissors.
Wood Mallet		

For all ordinary purposes these will be found sufficient, but an all-round jobbing hand working out-of-doors may find it necessary to supplement this list by a few extra tools.

The materials usually employed by the upholsterer are web, springs, canvas, horse-hair, fibres, wool and flocks, and coverings of various kinds.

Web.—This should be of British make; the sizes used generally are those known as Nos. 10, 12, and 14. The best results can be obtained with No. 14; it is more durable than the others, and also more expensive.

Springs.—These are drawn steel wire coppered, and are obtainable in sizes varying from 3 inches to 12 inches high. The gauge of wire is controlled by the nature of the work to be done; if the seat is to be hard, the stronger gauge spring will be used. They are wired together in half-dozens, and sold in 1 gross lots.

Spring Canvas.—This should be a heavy make of Hessian. One of the most frequent causes of a seat requiring re-doing is that an inferior canvas has been used, and the springs have broken through it. Canvas 72 inches wide will be found to cut up most economically. Canvas for outside backs or panel backs need not be of so heavy a quality.

Scrym.—This is a light make of canvas, open in texture, and is used for first stuffing purposes. A width of 36 inches is the best, but wider widths may be obtained.

Calico.—Gray unbleached calico free from dressing is required for second stuffing purposes; it should be 72 inches wide.

Black Canvas.—This is used for the underside of seats or outside backs not otherwise covered.

Wadding.—This is sold in gray, bleached, and black, in rolls of 12 yards long by about 30 inches wide. These waddings are skinned; the wadding used years ago was what is known as "pound wadding", which was without skin and sold by bulk. Of the above, gray wadding is that usually used, black wadding being suitable for putting under hair seating.

Tacks.—These should be cut, and used in sizes as under:—For webs, a tack known as $\frac{5}{8}$-inch improved tack; for first stuffing, canvas over springs, and most general purposes, a $\frac{1}{2}$-inch tack; for coverings, $\frac{3}{8}$ inch; for light pin-cushion backs a $\frac{1}{4}$-inch tack will be ample. The above will be blued steel, while for tacking on window-blinds tin tacks are required. All gimps, trimmings, &c., would be put on with gimp pins.

Twines.—These are commonly known as stitching, buttoning, and mattress, and should be all best hemp lines well laid, otherwise the constant friction of the twine passing through the canvas wastes both twine and time. Buttoning "twine" is a six-cord laid twine. The above are made up in $\frac{1}{2}$-lb. balls.

Horse-hair.—This is the best material for filling purposes, and is manufactured at prices varying from 6*d.* to 3*s.* per lb., the test of quality being its curl and the length of hair. The curl is produced by twisting into ropes about 1 inch in diameter, and curled hair is sold in this form. The only satisfactory way to open hair is by hand; all machine openers have a tendency to break the hair, thus taking away its elasticity. It can be had in black, gray, and white, but the last is not generally used.

Fibres.—There are a variety of these on the market, all equally good for first stuffing where hair cannot be used on account of the expense. Cocoa-nut fibre is generally used, and can be procured black with a mixture of hair. Alva (a kind of sea-weed) and wood fibre, consisting of very finely-cut pine shavings, are also used.

Wool and Flocks.—What is known in the trade as "wool" is usually shredded Kidderminster carpets, thoroughly cleansed and carded. Flocks should be mill waste and not torn-up rags. Care should always be taken, for hygienic reasons, that these materials are clean. They are usually used for mattresses rather than stuffing, as in the latter they do not keep their shape.

Coverings.—The variety of fabrics on the market to-day for the covering of furniture is endless, but a few general widths may be given. Velvets are 24 inches wide; also for curtains, &c., 36, 48, and 72 inches.   Silks, tapestries, damasks, and reps are 50 to 54 inches wide.   Hair seating is made every one inch from 18 to 36 inches wide.   Cretonnes are 30 inches wide, and chintz from 24 to 30 inches wide.

Skins.—Morocco, the skin of the goat, can be used with dull or hard grain, or embossed. The skins are dyed to any shade, and vary in size from 24 to 36 inches, the measurement being the mean width of the skin.   This is the best skin for the purposes of covering.

Roan is the skin of a sheep, and is treated as morocco, but as it is of a much softer nature it is used for outside backs, &c.

A morocco can be distinguished from a roan, as the former has a series of skin veins, which take the colour of the dye and stand out prominently on the back of the skin, while a roan has not.

American Leathers.—These are imitations of the real skin, and are sold in rolls 12 yards long by 45 inches wide, or, if purchased untrimmed, 48 inches wide.

First Stuffing.—We now come to the practical stuffing of a piece of furniture.   Let us suppose that we are to stuff a single chair.   The first operation on receiving the frame from the chair-maker will be to rasp down the upper and outer edge of the seat-rail to give a bed for the head of the tack when tacking down the scrym.   If this is not done, the head of the tack shows on the front when covered.   If the seat is spring stuffed, place the frame upside down upon a trestle, then tack on (after tightly straining) four webs from back to front, and four from side to side; do not stint the webbing if satisfactory work is desired, and do not use web strainers having either spikes or teeth.

We next proceed to attach the springs to the web.   The number of springs in a single chair may be either three, four, or five.   When only three are used, there is a tendency to throw the seated person entirely to the back of the chair, the weight consequently resting upon one spring; therefore four or five should be used.   The sizes may be 6 or 7 inches by medium gauge.   The springs should have three ties in each spring, separately knotted off, to be lashed on top both ways.   The covering canvas should be temporarily tacked at each corner, then tacked down each side and trimmed off, leaving, say, $\frac{3}{4}$ inch outside the tacks; this edge should be turned over toward the centre of the seat, and again tacked.   Three stitches in the form of a triangle on each spring complete the springing.   Proceed then to stitch twine in long stitches on the canvas to hold the hair for first stuffing; instead of stitching, the twine may be tacked on the frame in loops, and this is the better method. Then work under these the hair, which should be thoroughly opened and worked in firmly; this is of great importance, for if done properly it will not afterwards need "cramming". A little hair or wool should now be placed in the centre of the seat; the quantity of hair required for a small chair is $1\frac{1}{4}$ lb.   Now arrives the point at which the chair may be said to be made or marred, viz. the tacking down of the scrym preparatory to stitching. If more chairs than one are to be done, let all the scryms be cut the same size, usually 25 inches square.   Let the beginner draw one thread each way from the scrym; he can thus work to line, and so keep the job straight.   Put six tacks in each side, and with the needle run a series of stitches 3 inches from the edge of the seat through the spring canvas, not piercing the web.   In tacking down, turn in the scrym to the necessary length, and temporarily tack with $\frac{1}{2}$-inch tacks upon the edge previously rasped; commence this from the centre of each side, using additional hair if required.   This process should not be hurried, and make certain before driving home the tacks that it is of the desired weight and firmness; failing this, the edge when stitched will either hang over or hang in.   One blind and two top stitches are next worked round the edge of the chair, locking every third stitch by means of an extra twist round the needle.

Second Stuffing.—The chair is now ready for covering, plain or buttoned.   Say the latter.   Should this be a skin, it is marked as fig. 1052, No. 1, the best way of doing which is to draw upon a sheet of paper the desired plan of buttoning, afterwards stabbing through the skin at the points of intersection. No. 2 shows the method of marking where more skins than one are required, as in continuous seating. Paste a piece of Holland to counteract the button tension. On the seat itself draw a central line from back to front, and another at right angles about 2 inches from the front, thus forming the basis for marking the buttons. Next cut the scrym diagonally about $\frac{3}{4}$ inch, and with the finger clear away the hair to allow the button to sink. With buttoning twine stitch down to the spring canvas, leaving both ends loose on the seat. Then string the seat diagonally between the buttons in similar manner as in first stuffing, and work under the hair. Lay on wadding over all and draw the button strings through. The skin, having been marked and creased, is ready to be put on. This operation should be commenced at the centre by passing

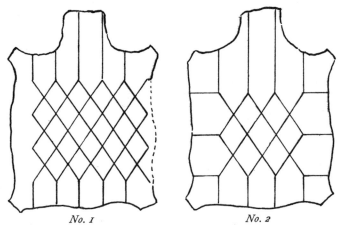

No. 1   No. 2

Fig. 1052.—Skins marked for Buttoning: No. 1, for chair; No. 2, for seating

the buttoning string through it and the button. In passing it through the latter, see that the twine is put through the button canvas diagonally; this gives double the strength. Finish off each diamond separately, forming each plait with a regulator, until the seat is completed. Clear the edge from all loose hair, and tack down. It is then ready for finishing off with banding or other trimming. Tie off the twine beneath the button, and pass the loose end through the seat.

The same process would take place exactly in stuffing and covering easy-chairs or couches, except in the case of spring edges, the method of doing which would be as follows:— Inside the front rail strain a web from side to side, cover the front rail with felt, and stitch on, say, 6-inch springs, leaving 1 inch between each; tie to the top edges of these a split cane or piece of spring wire, thus connecting them together; then by means of strips of web run through the middle coil of the spring, draw the edge well over the front rail, and tack off; sew a piece of canvas to the seat canvas, draw over the springs and tack on front rail, sewing the cane or wire edge and springs firmly to it; work in the hair and place over scrym as for a small chair, stitching just below the wire edge with one blind and one top stitch; the seat would then be finished in the ordinary way.

The usual allowance on a flat surface for fulness would be about one quarter more than the finished size of the diamond. Thus, a diamond marked 11 inches by $8\frac{3}{4}$ inches would finish 9 inches by 7 inches; on the round (such as the scroll of a couch) much more fulness will be required, varying according to the quickness of the sweep. A greater amount of fulness would be necessary in fabrics on account of forming a deeper plait.

In plain work the first stuffing would be as previously described. String the seat, work on $\frac{3}{4}$ lb. of best hair and cover with calico, then with wadding, and tack on the covering, cutting for the back legs by turning over the cover and cutting from the apex of the angle at 45° to the inside edge of leg. Should the covering be leather, before putting on the wadding tie down the seat by running it through with buttoning twine, each stitch passing through the webs; thoroughly strain the skin and release the ties; the seat will then spring up and tighten the skin, thus preventing it stretching afterwards.

CHAPTER V

SHOP-FITTING

1. *External Fittings.*—During the last decade the man of business has been impressed with the facts that, if he would keep abreast of the times, he must make an attractive display of the goods he has to sell, and that nothing conduces so much towards this end as an attractive shop front. The materials used by the shop-fitter may be either metal or wood. The former, while possessing many advantages, has its corresponding disadvantages. It may be brass, copper, steel, or an amalgam, but all these metals need a daily expense in cleaning and polishing to keep them in good order, of which the proprietor soon tires; and if a metal front is in a manufacturing or chemical district, the polluted atmosphere soon affects it, and the final result is most unsatisfactory. Therefore we turn to such work as can be manufactured in wood, and our first consideration is what timbers are available for the purpose, and which is most suitable.

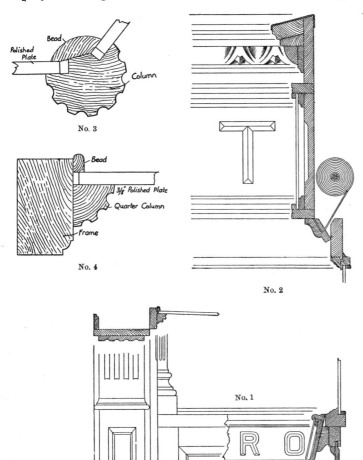

Fig. 1053.—Details of Shop Front: No. 1, Plans, Elevation, and Section of Lower Part; No. 2, Elevation and Section of Upper Part; No. 3, Angle-column; No. 4, Quarter Column and Frame

Among the hardwoods which may be used are—Teak, Oak, Mahogany, and Walnut.

These are placed in their order of durability for outside work, and teak above all woods seems for many reasons to be the beau-ideal for the purpose; it does not shrink or swell, warp or open, and exposure to the atmosphere hardens and solidifies it. The other woods are liable in varying degree to climatic influences, and very old seasoned timber would have to be selected to meet with the full measure of success.

The usual demand made upon the shop-fitter is that he shall design a front " all glass and no wood ", that is to say, that every available inch shall be given to the window-space, and the wood-work reduced almost to vanishing point. This condition somewhat handicaps the designer, as it allows little room for panelling, mouldings, &c., and the columns in the window-angles must be much too slender to be architecturally correct.

Plate LXXVII gives an ordinary double-fronted shop with revolving spring sun-blind, sign-boards, and lettered and glazed fascia sign. The following should be noted in connection with the detail drawings.

PLATE LXXVII

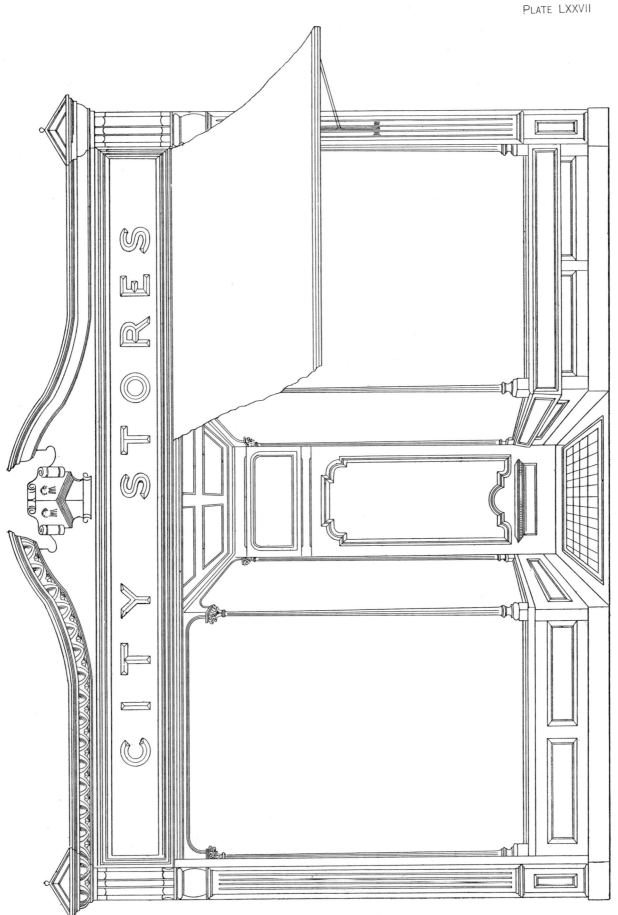

CITY STORES

SHOP-FRONT

Framework (fig. 1053).—It will be found that a breadth of 3 inches will be ample for ordinary requirements, employed thus:—Sill 3 inches × 3 inches, top rail 3 inches × 2 inches, uprights 3 inches × 2 inches. These should be mortised and tenoned and wedged, and put together with a little white-lead; as an additional safeguard a few screws may be used. The framework at the angle should be secured by bed-bolts 6 inches × $\frac{3}{8}$ inch. The side frames should be fixed with good steel screws into wedges driven into the brickwork.

If the sill is to be covered by a name-board, it is not necessary to mould it, a plain chamfer being all that is required. The panels beneath the sill may be of wood, or if a cellar is under the shop, obscured glass is usually put in. The plinth should be of marble or stone; wood is soon spoilt by the feet of shop-gazers.

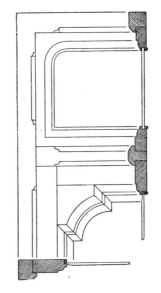

The angle columns (No. 3) should be in three pieces made to dowel together, with two dowels to each joint. (1) The capital should be cut from $3\frac{1}{2}$ inches to 5 inches in length and roughly turned in the lathe to the required shape, which can then be more easily opened up and finished by the carver; the neck members must be made to suit the diameter of the shaft. (2) The shaft may vary from $1\frac{1}{4}$ to $1\frac{3}{4}$ inch in diameter according to the height, and may be either a plain round, or fluted. The fluted column is lighter and more graceful. (3) The base is turned in the lathe (say) 5 inches deep, and is housed and dowelled into the sill.

The door (fig. 1054) should be framed up in 2-inch stuff, and if rebated should be hung on three $4\frac{1}{2}$-inch steel-washered butts. The upper panel should be glazed; $\frac{1}{4}$-inch polished plate with 1-inch bevel is very suitable. The fanlight should be made to open, a gun-metal opener, such as Cartmell's, being fixed for the purpose.

Sign-boards are made in an infinite variety. Very often an engraved brass or copper plate mounted upon a moulded board suffices. The sign of which a section is shown in No. 2, fig. 1053, is what is known as an incised gilt and glazed sign. This kind is by far the most durable and perfectly dust-proof, and can hardly be beaten for effect. The letters should be cut at least $\frac{1}{2}$ inch into the hardwood back, and gilt in leaf; the edging is rebated for the glass ($\frac{1}{4}$-inch polished plate), and put on in lead.

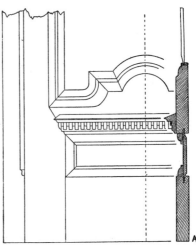

Fig. 1054.—Details of Door

Sun-blind.—For this purpose a 3-inch tin-spring barrel-roller should be used and fixed behind the sign, as shown in the detail (No. 2, fig. 1053). Great care must be taken that it is coiled sufficiently before fixing and that it runs perfectly plumb; this should be ascertained by a level. The covering should be linen tick that has been made damp-proof.

Show-space.—Ordinary tongued and grooved 1-inch boards laid on 3-inch × 2-inch joists will, as a rule, suffice for the floor of the show-space. If the window back is to be enclosed, it can be done by sliding glazed doors with brass rollers running on a steel plate; or an air-tight enclosure may be formed.

A design for a shop front suitable for a milliner's or general draper's shop is shown in fig. 1055. This represents one of a series of shops built in the picturesque Chester Rows. Lightness of construction and abundance of plate glass have been pushed to their extreme limit in this design, which gives a *maximum* of space for show purposes with a *minimum* of waste.

2. *Interior Fittings.*—The nature and design of the interior fittings of a shop vary according to locality and the nature of the articles sold. Fruiterers and florists are content with plain wooden fittings. Fishmongers, poulterers, and butchers have their fittings constructed of marble slabs resting on glazed brick or tiled supports, and usually have a small interior office of wood and glass. Chemists, jewellers, opticians, booksellers, and stationers are likewise modest in their requirements. The greatest scope for the display

Fig. 1055.—Shop Front at Chester

of elaborate fittings and plate-glass is afforded by the shops of large drapers and fashionable *modistes*.

The back of a shop window may be enclosed by sliding doors glazed with plain plate or ornamental glass, or it may be shut off by a glazed partition fitted with one or more hinged doors, but the nature of the arrangement depends upon the shape of the shop front and the kind of articles to be shown. Some shop windows, those of tailors in particular, are enclosed by a partition rising only a few feet above the level of the shop front. This partition may be constructed with framework and panels wholly in wood, or it may be partly glazed. Mirrors are often fitted in some of the panels. The top is usually finished with a moulding, and may be level or shaped in various ways. Mahogany, oak, or walnut 1 inch thick are employed for window-backs, but the framework is sometimes 2 inches thick. A simple window-back is constructed by hanging a curtain of coloured cloth on a brass rod supported on wood or brass pillars. The interior of the window is fitted according to the requirements of the proprietor. Some windows are left bare of fittings for the display of goods, whilst others are provided with shelves. The floor is sometimes built up in the form of steps rising one behind the other.

Counters vary so much in dimensions and general design that it is impossible to give designs and details to meet every case. In drapers' shops they are usually about $2\frac{1}{2}$ feet wide and high. Fig. 1056 is an illustration of a counter with shelves and cupboards behind that might be required by stationers, &c. The framing of the counter may vary from 1 to

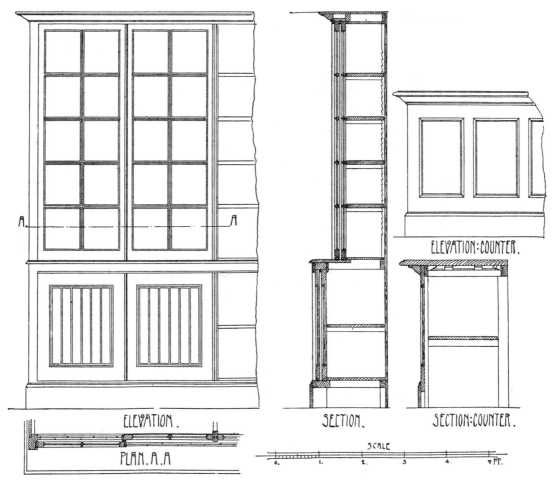

Fig. 1056.—Counter and Shelves, &c., for a Shop

$1\frac{1}{2}$ inch in thickness, and the panels from $\frac{3}{8}$ to $\frac{1}{2}$ inch; the latter may be plain boards, or tongued-and-grooved boards with chamfered edges, and fitted vertically or diagonally. The edge of the top is fitted with a moulding, as are also the panels, and the lower part with a moulded plinth or skirting. The top of the counter varies from 1 to $1\frac{1}{2}$ inch in thickness, and is usually of baywood or other hardwood, which can be obtained in wide boards. For supports, a transverse framework made of stuff about 2 inches thick is fitted every few feet, or the whole counter is built on to a framework made of scantling. One or two shelves are fitted underneath if required, and sometimes there is a range of drawers immediately under the counter-top. If necessary, part of the counter-top is made to lift up by being hinged, while a corresponding part of the front is hinged so that it swings inwards.

The shelves on the wall behind the counter are made of $\frac{3}{4}$- or 1-inch material according to the span and width. They are supported every 3 or 4 feet by turned pillars or by side pieces from 1 to $1\frac{1}{2}$ inch thick, into which they are housed. They may be protected from dust, &c., by sliding doors, which should be fitted with rollers to slide on grooves fitted with strips of metal. The old-fashioned hinged doors are still much used, although not so convenient. The wall behind the shelves is usually covered with ½- or ¾-inch match-boarding nailed to ¾-inch grounds.

Nests of drawers are sometimes fitted in the shelving, the drawers being separated by ½- or 1-inch boards. The fronts of the drawers may be of mahogany or other hard wood, or of some inferior wood painted or covered with dark-green paper or bookbinder's cloth. The drawers are provided with one or two brass handles, or with hardwood, brass, or china knobs. A cornice is fixed at the top of the shelving. The "carved" members in these cornices are sometimes made by passing lengths of mould-ing, of the requisite size and softened by steam, be-tween steel rollers upon which the pattern is cut. There is a projecting shelf at the level of the counter; the space below this is fitted with shelves, and either left open or closed with sliding doors.

Fig. 1057.—Counter and Fittings for a Bank

More elaborate fittings suitable for a bank or office are shown in fig. 1057. In shops such as those of perfumers, confectioners, and hair-dressers, the counter fronts sometimes have panels of bevelled plate-glass. The fronts of some counters are also fitted with a small projecting ledge of curved section about 4 or 5 inches wide for umbrellas, parcels, &c. This is made of a net of cord or wire fastened to a brass rod from 1 to 1½ inch in diameter, supported by brass brackets.

Cashiers' Boxes are usually square or hexagonal, entered by a door at the side or back. They have a stout framework, which is panelled below, but glazed above the level of the desk-at which the clerk sits.

CHAPTER VI

SIDEBOARDS, BOOK-CASES, AND CABINETS

Sideboards consist of a lower part which contains cupboards, drawers, and a cellarette, and above this there is often an upper part fitted with mirrors, cupboards, and shelves for ornaments or plate. Sideboards may be divided roughly into those which are heavy and

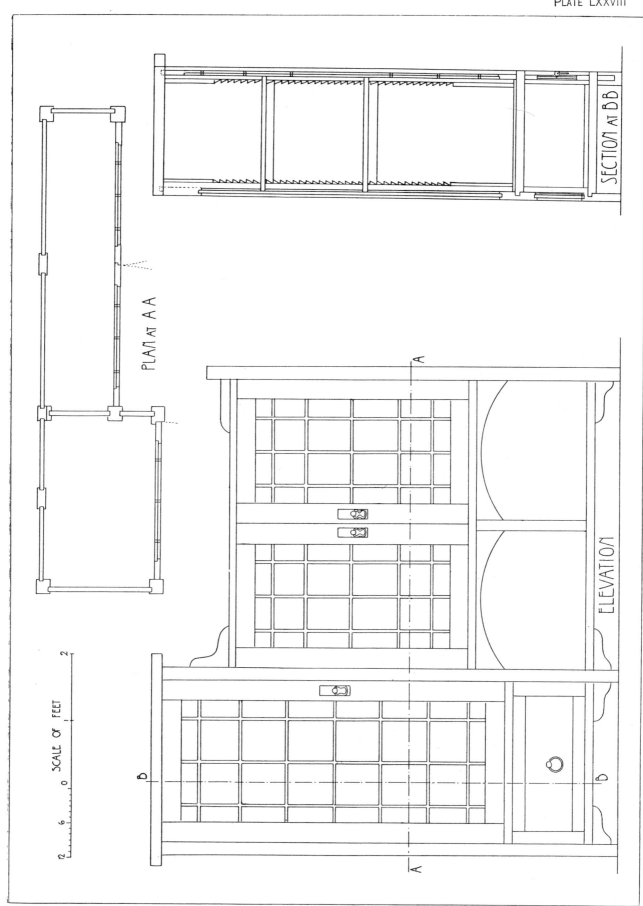

PLATE LXXVIII

SECTION AT BB

PLAN AT AA

SCALE OF FEET

ELEVATION

DESIGN FOR BOOKCASE

massive, and those which are lighter in construction and intended for small rooms. All large sideboards ought to be so designed that they can be easily taken to pieces for removal.

The simplest kind of heavy sideboard has a range of three drawers resting upon two cupboards or "pedestals", 2, 3, or more feet apart. These cupboards are closed by doors, fitted with shelves, and raised about 6 inches above the floor. A ledge of $\frac{1}{2}$-inch wood is sometimes fastened round the shelves, and these fit into grooves cut in the sides of the cupboard, so that they can be pulled out. Extra grooves may be added so that the distance between the shelves can be altered. The top is left quite plain, but its edge is curved, moulded, beaded, or carved. A mirror mounted in a frame may be fastened to the back of the top. The space between the cupboards may be fitted with a tier of drawers or another cupboard. The cupboard doors may be partly glazed with opaque coloured glass mounted in lead frames. An improved effect is obtained by using antique metal hinges and key-plates for the doors, and similar handles for the drawers. Several smaller bevelled mirrors may be mounted instead of a large one at the back, and the space between the mirrors fitted with shelves supported on brackets or turned and fluted pillars. There may be a large mirror with a smaller one on either side of it, or a mirror may be mounted on one half of the back and the other half fitted with a cupboard and closed by a glazed door. Similarly, the regularity of the lower part may be relieved by inserting a cupboard on one side and drawers on the other, or drawers above, then a cupboard, and another range of drawers below.

Plates LXXIX to LXXXII contain designs for a sideboard and book-case by Mr. Talwin Morris. The details given in Plate LXXXI explain the methods of setting out the work, &c. The book-case was designed to contain specified volumes and portfolios, and at the same time to fill its appointed wall space. It and the sideboard are constructed in Austrian oak stained and polished to tone with other furniture. The doors are leaded with clear glass relieved by spots of colour. The key-plates, panels, and other fittings are in beaten and bronzed brass.

Plates LXXXIII and LXXXIV contain an elevation, section, plan, and details of a sideboard designed by the editor to fit a shallow recess in a small but lofty dining-room. The lower part projects beyond the wall-line, and the corners are rounded for convenience in passing. This portion contains cupboards, the lower of which has a flap-door, curved in section and hinged at the bottom. The cupboard above this has doors hinged at the side in the usual way. Above the "top" of the sideboard there is another cupboard supported on turned columns, the back and elbows between the sideboard top and the cupboard being formed with panelled framing. The panels of this framing and of the cupboard doors above are filled with "vitremur"—a kind of opaque coloured glass—in lead cames. The sideboard was constructed of oak fumed to match some old oak chairs in the same room. The hinges, escutcheons, &c., are of "antique" copper.

When furnishing libraries in large houses, book-cases are built of such a height and width that they cover most of the wall space. Such book-cases often have an upper part about 1 foot deep, and resting upon a lower part which projects 6 inches beyond it to form a ledge about $2\frac{1}{2}$ or 3 feet from the floor. A cornice is fitted round the top edge of the upper part. The lower part is usually fitted partly with shelves and partly with cupboards, or only with shelves, according to requirements. In the commoner book-cases of this kind there are usually no doors, and the front edges of the shelves are left plain or covered with an edging of leather fastened with ornamental brass-headed nails or with a wood fillet. In the superior kinds sliding or hinged doors are used. These may be glazed with plain or bevelled plate-glass in single sheets, or may be divided into smaller panes of various shapes by means of sash-bars. Sometimes opaque glass is used. The sash-bars are generally curved in book-cases of Chippendale and Sheraton design, and in the lighter and more elegant pieces of furniture intended for drawing-rooms.

The book-cases in public libraries do not always have glazed doors; the glass is replaced by a net- or trellis-work made of brass wire of $\frac{1}{8}$ inch diameter, the wires being fastened diagonally with about 2 inches space between each.

Grooves are cut at short distances apart across the inside of the end-pieces, so that the distance between the shelves can be altered according to requirements. There are, however, several methods of adjusting this distance. The most convenient way is to cut notches along the edges of two strips of wood $\frac{1}{2}$ inch thick and about $1\frac{1}{2}$ inch wide, and long enough to extend from top to bottom of the row of shelves. The notches have approximately the same shape as those forming the teeth of a saw. One of these strips is fastened to the interior of the framing at each corner of the shelving, the notches pointing inwards. Pieces of wood about $1\frac{1}{2}$ inch wide and $\frac{1}{2}$ inch thick are cut at the ends so that they will just fit across the ends of the book-case between the notches. These can be adjusted at any height by simply removing and reinserting in the proper position. Both ends of each shelf are notched out $\frac{1}{2}$ by $1\frac{1}{2}$ inch at each corner so that they will move up and down between the notched strips. Of course the notches must correspond at each end of the bookcase.

Another method of adjusting the shelves is to bore two vertical rows of holes inside each end of the book-case, these holes being of $\frac{3}{8}$ inch diameter, $\frac{1}{2}$ inch deep, 1 inch apart, and 2 inches from the front or back. Wooden pegs may be fitted into these holes to support the shelves, or, better still, metal bureau shelf-pins. These consist of a piece of metal 1 inch wide and $\frac{1}{4}$ inch thick bent at right angles, and provided with a round shank which exactly fits the hole. A groove 1 inch wide and $\frac{1}{4}$ inch deep must be ploughed down each line of holes to prevent the metal getting in the way of the books. Tonk's shelf-fitting consists of a long strip of iron pierced with a series of rectangular holes, into which small projecting pieces of metal fit and support the shelves. An appliance known as Chiver's wedge-and-shelf bracket is very useful for the same purpose. The bracket slides in a groove made at the ends of the book-case, and is held in any position by two wedges, of which one has a serrated edge. When it is desired to alter its position, one of the wedges is loosened, and it can then be slid to any height and fixed by tightening the wedge.

Book-cases of the ordinary kind are usually made in two parts, an upper and a lower, which are fastened together by several screws passing downwards through the bottom of the upper part. The latter may consist of nothing but shelves; it may also be provided with one or more cupboards. A carved or moulded cornice is fastened round the top. The lower portion projects about 6 or 9 inches beyond the upper; its top edge is moulded, and a plinth may be fitted round the lower, or the whole may be raised on feet so that the lowest shelf or "bottom" is 6 inches or more from the floor. This lower portion may be provided with shelves only, with a combination of shelves, cupboards, and drawers, or with a bureau drawer at the top and cupboards below. The shelves are covered with one or more doors.

There is as much variety in the design of bookcases as in that of sideboards. When the book-case is only 3 or 4 feet wide the upper part is usually of uniform depth, but when the width is greater the uniformity of the front is often broken up, either by recessing the middle part, or by recessing the two ends and letting the middle project. The middle part is usually rather wider than the two ends. The lower part may be of uniform depth, or recessed to match the upper, a projecting ledge 6 inches wide being left all along the front. Some book-cases are constructed with open recesses or shelves for china, &c. Dwarf book-cases are made in one piece, and only 3 or 4 feet high, standing on four short legs, or being supported on a plinth. The top is highly finished, and can be embellished with china, &c.

The details of construction vary according to the design. In constructing the lower part of more massive book-cases a framework is made by fastening perpendicular lengths of scantling 2 inches square to the plinth, which forms the base, or to a lower shelf 1 or $1\frac{1}{2}$ inch thick. These pieces of scantling form the corner-pieces, and intermediate rails are inserted with mortise-and-tenon joints to add strength. The top of the lower part is made of 1-inch boards dowelled together, and usually projects 2 or 3 inches over the front and sides. The back and sides are formed with plain boarding, or the sides (if exposed) may be framed and panelled. If the middle part is recessed, four extra pieces of scantling must be added, two being at the front and two in an intermediate position. Boards are also fastened across from back to front at the places where the recess is made to form the divisions between the compartments. The upper part is made in the same manner, and either screwed down flush with the lower, or into a slight hollow made for it by fixing strips of half-round or squared wood in the right position. In large movable book-cases, each compartment should be complete in itself, so that the whole can be easily taken to pieces for removal. For this purpose each compartment is made with ends; thus, in the case of a book-case with three compartments and in two heights, there will be six distinct nests of shelves. The divisions between the central and side compartments will obviously be double, and the joint is masked by a facing fixed to one of the two boards. The "top" of the lower part is made in one piece, as joints would be unsightly, and is fixed to the framing with screws. The cornice of the upper part is treated in a similar manner.

Plate LXXVIII shows the front elevation, section, and plan of a book-case suitable for the corner of a library or some position in a hall. The higher part has three tiers of shelves, with a drawer below this tier; the lower book-case stands on framing, forming two alcoves. These are suitable for china or large works of reference. The main uprights are 2 inches square, and the back and sides are made of 1-inch framing, into which ½-inch panels are tongued and grooved.

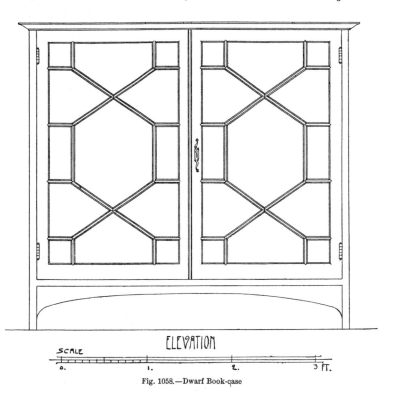

ELEVATION

SCALE

Fig. 1058.—Dwarf Book-case

Fig. 1058 is a design for a dwarf book-case suitable for a drawing-room. It is about 3 feet high, 4 feet wide, and 1 foot deep. The case is composed of a rectangular framework of 1-inch boards, which form the top, bottom, and sides. Horizontal rails are fastened to these, and the intervening space filled with panels to form the back. The supports may be made longer, and a drawer added under the bookcase. The glass is fitted into rebates in the wood frames and bars, and is plain, bevelled, or coloured according to taste. When the panes of glass are inserted in their places, they are fixed by putty, or by strips of wood about ¼-inch thick sprigged or glued round the inside of the rebate, and mitred at the angles. Dwarf book-cases may be finished off with buhl-work or marqueterie.

Plans, elevations, and section of an eight-door book-case with upper and lower portions are shown in fig. 1059. The front of the lower part is built on to four pieces of scantling about 2 inches square; these are connected by the bottom board, which forms the lowest shelf, and another board, which forms the top. The upper front is similarly constructed. The back has an upright at each end, and two intermediate uprights; these are connected by horizontal rails of 1-inch stuff, and the intermediate spaces are filled by ½-inch

panels grooved into the framing.   The back and front are joined by 1-inch boards, but
if lightness of construction is essential, the ends may be panelled.   The doors are hinged
to the uprights, and the left-hand doors of the middle part are fitted with vertical bolts
at the top and bottom, by which they are fastened, and the fellow doors to these are closed
by ordinary bolts worked by turning the handles.   The top is made of $\frac{1}{2}$-inch stuff, and a

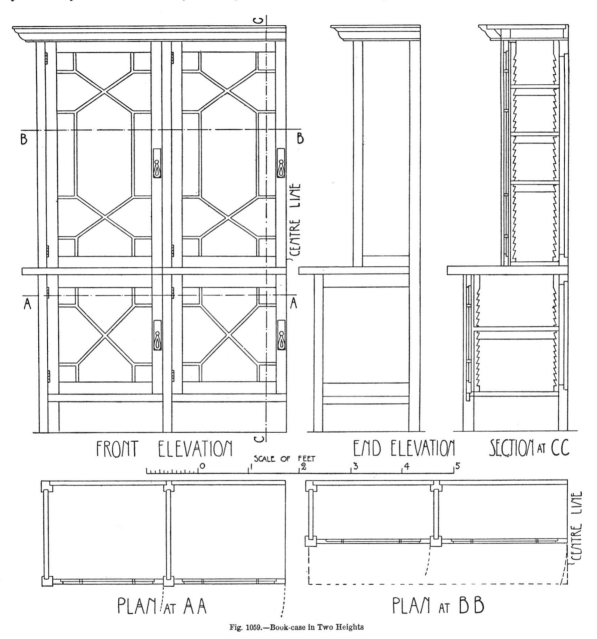

Fig. 1059.—Book-case in Two Heights

slanting board is fastened to the front and sides, and to this the moulding which forms
the cornice is attached by passing screws from the inside.   As this moulding forms a
receptacle for dust, &c., it is best to cover the top with another $\frac{1}{2}$-inch board.

Revolving Book-cases.—No. 1, fig. 1060, is an illustration of a completed revolving
book-case of the ordinary type.   It stands 3 or 4 feet high, and is about 20 inches square.
A plan of the base on which the book-case revolves is shown on No. 2.   This is made
of two pieces of wood $2\frac{1}{2}$ inches wide and $1\frac{1}{2}$ inch thick.   These are joined together
by halving, and have rounded ends.   Four castors are fixed to the base, one near each
corner.   The top is made of $1\frac{1}{2}$-inch boards dowelled together, and the edge moulded and

PLATE LXXIX

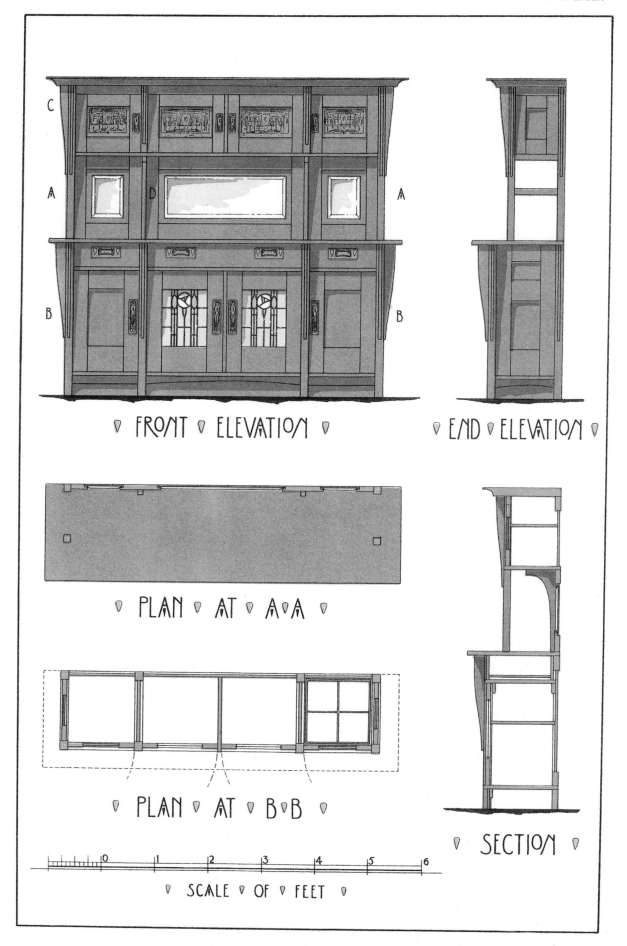

FRONT ▽ ELEVATION

END ▽ ELEVATION

C

A   D   A

B   B

PLAN ▽ AT ▽ A ▽ A

PLAN ▽ AT ▽ B ▽ B

SECTION

0   1   2   3   4   5   6

SCALE ▽ OF ▽ FEET

DESIGN FOR DINING-ROOM SIDEBOARD

PLATE LXXX

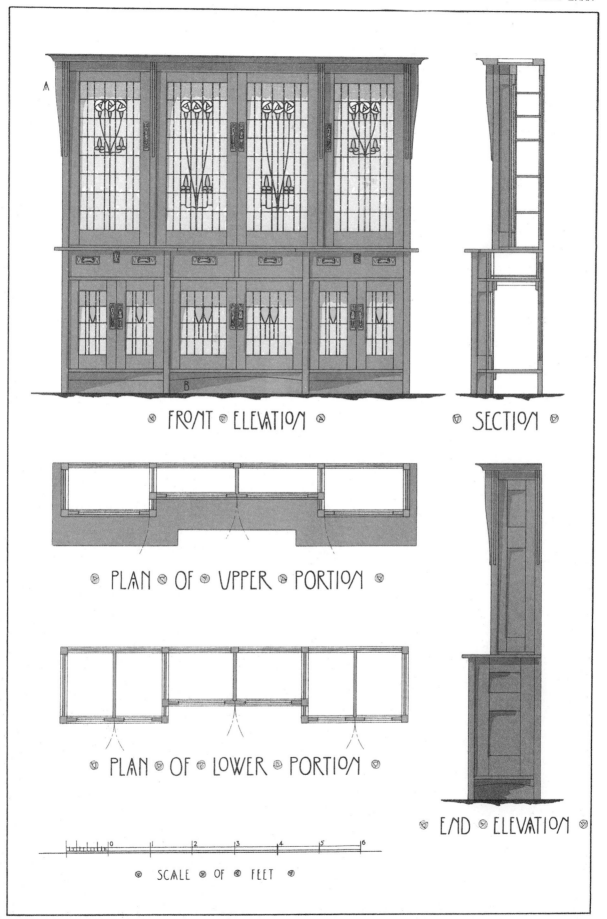

A

B

◉ FRONT ◉ ELEVATION ◉

◉ SECTION ◉

◉ PLAN ◉ OF ◉ UPPER ◉ PORTION ◉

◉ PLAN ◉ OF ◉ LOWER ◉ PORTION ◉

◉ END ◉ ELEVATION ◉

0   1   2   3   4   5   6

◉ SCALE ◉ OF ◉ FEET ◉

DESIGN FOR BOOKCASE

PLATE LXXXI

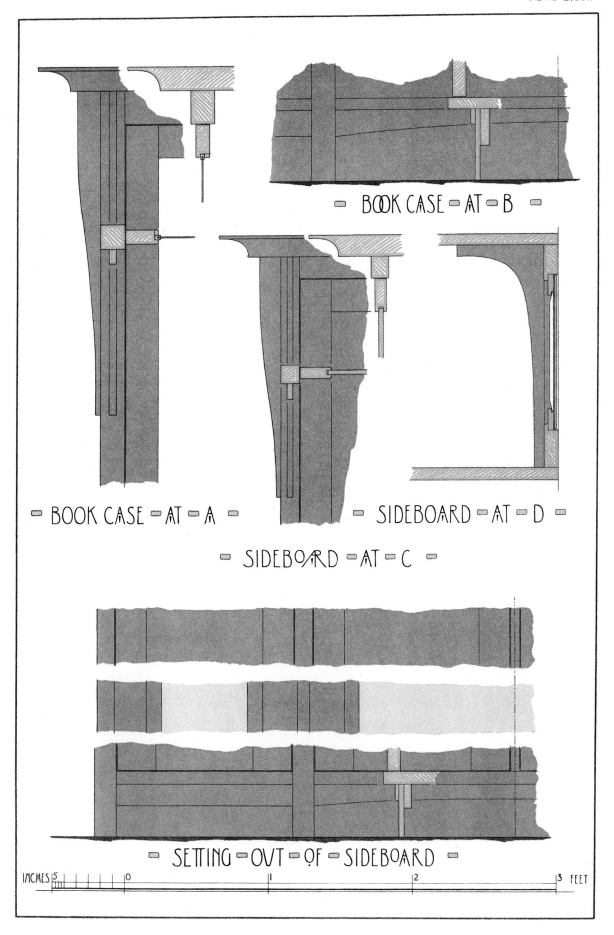

- BOOK CASE - AT - B -

- BOOK CASE - AT - A -

- SIDEBOARD - AT - D -

- SIDEBOARD - AT - C -

- SETTING - OUT - OF - SIDEBOARD -

INCHES 5   0   1   2   3 FEET

DETAILS OF BOOKCASE AND SIDEBOARD

PLATE LXXXII

VIEWS OF BOOK-CASE AND SIDEBOARD (SEE PLATES LXXIX AND LXXX)

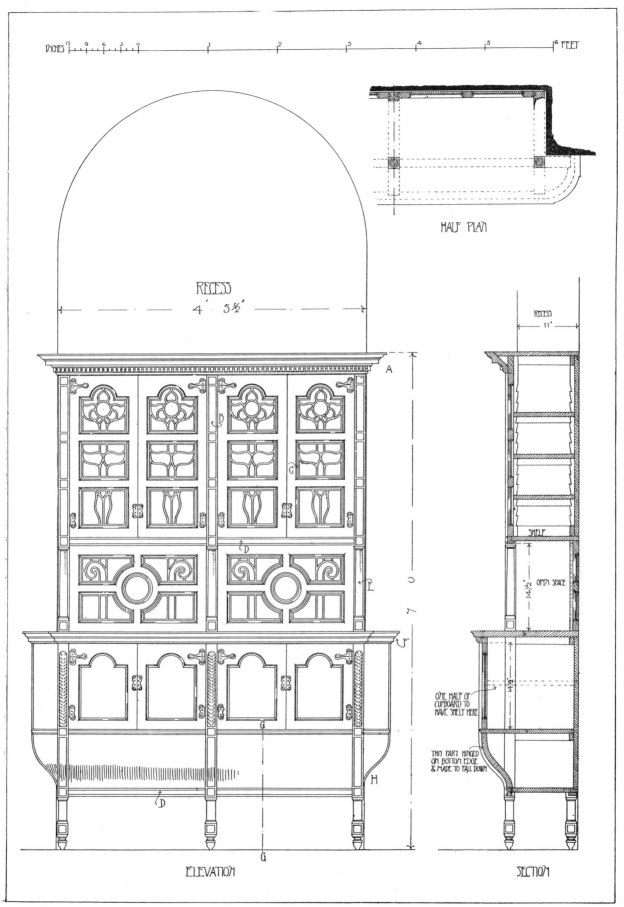

Plate· LXXXIII

INCHES 12 9 6 3 0   1   2   3   4   5   6 FEET

HALF PLAN

RECESS
4' 5½'

RECESS
11"

SHELF

14½" OPEN SPACE

14½"

ONE HALF OF
CUPBOARD TO
HAVE SHELF HERE

THIS PART HINGED
ON BOTTOM EDGE
& MADE TO FALL DOWN

ELEVATION

SECTION

Designed by G. Lister Sutcliffe, A.R.I.B.A.

OAK SIDEBOARD

PLATE LXXXIV

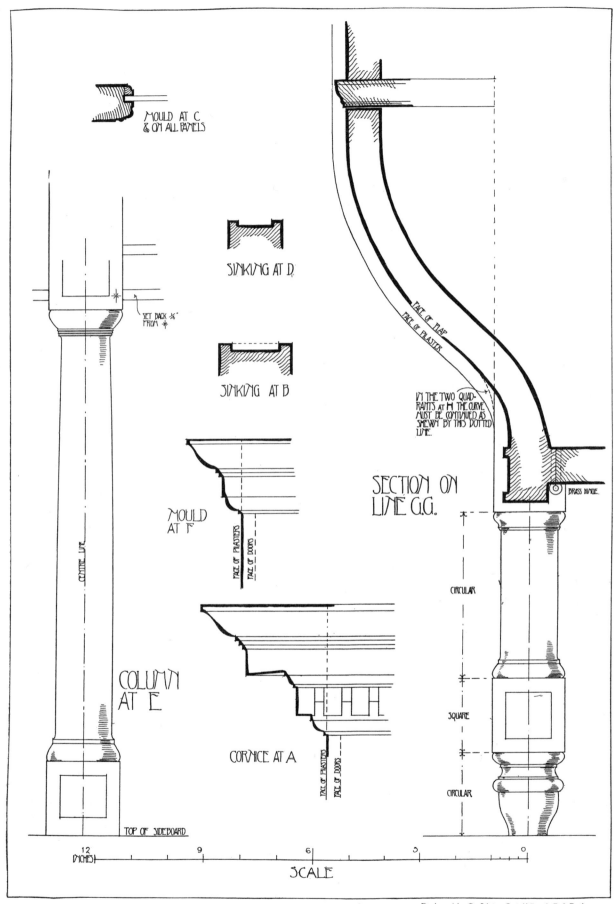

MOULD AT C
& ON ALL PANELS

SINKING AT D.

SINKING AT B

SET BACK ¼"
FROM

MOULD
AT F

FACE OF PLASTERS
FACE OF DOORS

COLUMN
AT E

CORNICE AT A

FACE OF PLASTERS
FACE OF DOORS

CENTRE LINE

TOP OF SIDEBOARD

FACE OF FLAP
FACE OF PLASTER

SECTION ON
LINE G.G.

IN THE TWO QUAD-
RANTS AT H THE CURVE
MUST BE CONTINUED AS
SHEWN BY THIS DOTTED
LINE.

BRASS HINGE.

CIRCULAR

SQUARE

CIRCULAR

12
INCHES   9   6   5   0

SCALE

Designed by G. Lister Sutcliffe, A.R.I.B.A.

DETAILS OF OAK SIDEBOARD

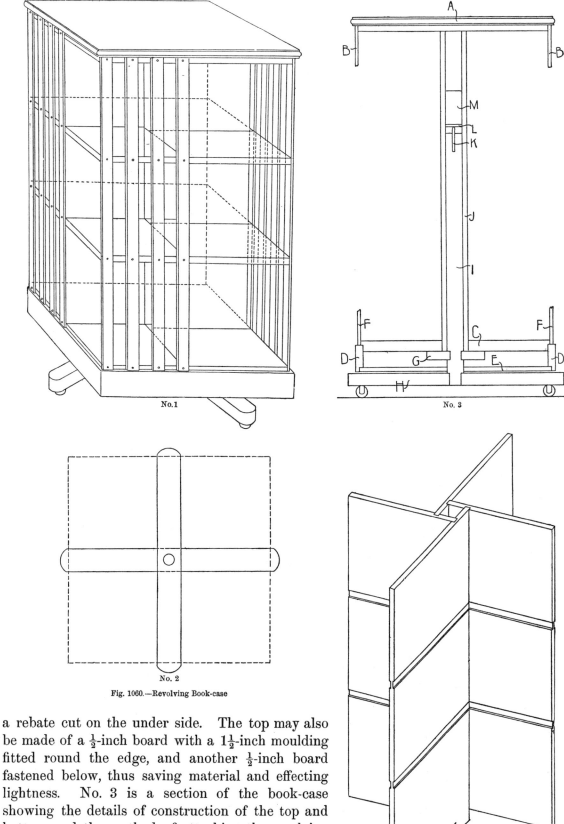

No.1

No. 3

No. 2

Fig. 1060.—Revolving Book-case

No.4

a rebate cut on the under side. The top may also be made of a ½-inch board with a 1½-inch moulding fitted round the edge, and another ½-inch board fastened below, thus saving material and effecting lightness. No. 3 is a section of the book-case showing the details of construction of the top and bottom and the method of attaching the revolving part to the base, A being the top, B F and B F two of the laths which keep the books in position, and H the fixed base (shown in No. 2). The base of the revolving part is made of 1½-inch boards, C, which have a rebate cut round the lower edge to receive the 1-inch plinth, D D, which is mitred at the corners and fastened into the rebate. The lower edge of the plinth is rebated and a thin board, E, fixed into it.

No. 4 is a perspective view of the frame to which the shelves are fastened. It is made of four boards of equal width and thickness joined by grooves and overlapping so that a square tube is formed. These boards must be of such a width that, when fastened in their places, the width of the frame is the same as that of the base, C (No. 3). The middle part of the frame should be 1½ inch longer than the rest, and fit into the centre of C. Another way of fastening the shelves, which requires less material, is to make a square tube, and attach the shelves to this. Strips of wood 2 or 3 inches wide are fastened along the top and bottom of each shelf in the position in which the boards (No. 4) would come. These strips keep the books in position at one end of each row, and the laths (B F and B F, No. 3) at the other end.

The method of pivoting the revolving part is shown in No. 3. A circular pillar, I, is turned to fit the interior of the square tube, and the lower end is turned down to form a

Fig. 1061.—Japanese Cabinet

pivot which fits the hole in the fixed base, H; a little above the pivot a groove is cut in the pillar, forming a neck which works in a hole cut in a piece of 1-inch board, G, which is attached to the under side of C. This piece of wood is sawn in half, the two halves placed in position on the pillar, and then glued together again. The pillar extends to within about a foot of the top of the tube. A steel spindle, K, with a pointed top is screwed into the upper end, and this spindle pivots in the under side of a metal plate, L, which is attached to a block of wood, M. The latter should exactly fit the tube, and is attached to it by screws.

The revolving apparatus can also be made by fastening two or more castors or wheels to the lower side of the base. These castors roll over a metal plate fastened to the upper side of the fixed base. The latter is attached to the revolving part by a spindle, which passes through the frame and the base, and is secured by nuts.

When the top and bottom have been attached to the tube, and the shelves are in their places, the laths B F and B F (No. 3) are attached to the shelves, and also to the rebates at the top and bottom, by brass-headed nails or screws.

Revolving book-cases may be circular or hexagonal instead of square, the principles of construction being essentially the same. Sometimes the revolving part is made shorter, and legs added to the fixed base. They are also made to contain only one tier of books, so that they can stand on the table. Fixed book-stands are also made with shelves arranged similarly to the revolving book-cases.

Cabinets.—Cabinets are, according to size, design, and finish, suitable for the hall, dining-room, or drawing-room. Heavy massive cabinets of carved oak or walnut are sometimes placed in halls, and serve to keep hats and cloaks, or for the display of china. Similar pieces of furniture are used in dining-rooms for the display of china and curios, but it is in reception- and drawing-rooms that the finest specimens are to be found. They have, as a rule, one or more doors enclosing shelves, and a few drawers and open spaces. They are finished with polish, black stain picked out with gold, and embellished with brass fittings, buhl-work, or marqueterie. The finest cabinets are decorated with bas-relief carvings, which may be executed in light wood.

Fig. 1061 is from a photograph of a Japanese cabinet suitable for a hall or dining-room. The cabinet itself is 3 feet square, and is supported on a carved table $2\frac{1}{2}$ feet high, of Renaissance design. The cabinet is made of 1-inch material, with the exception of the back, which is thinner. The interior, which is closed by two doors, is fitted with a series of drawers of different sizes and separated from one another by $\frac{3}{8}$-inch boards. A light ring-shaped handle is attached to each drawer. The inside and outside of the doors, the fronts of the drawers, and the exterior are decorated with bronzed lacquer-work, as shown in the illustration. The outside is further embellished with ornamental brass hinges, key-plates, and corner-pieces.

Fig. 1062 is an illustration of a drawing-room cabinet, stained black and finished with brass. It is 4 feet high, $5\frac{1}{2}$ feet long, and $1\frac{1}{2}$ foot deep. The lower part rests on a framework made of four rails, and strengthened by additional cross-pieces. Under this are fixed four short turned feet which fit into sockets. The two round fluted pillars in the middle portion, and the square pillars at the ends, are fastened to the lower frame and to an upper framework which carries the top. The central door is finished plain black inside, and with buhl-work and brasswork outside. The two side doors are made of $\frac{3}{4}$-inch stuff, curved

Fig. 1062.—Dwarf Drawing-room Cabinet

to match the curve of the base and top. There are two shelves in each of the end compartments and one in the middle; these are covered with crimson plush, as are also the sides and back. Drawing-room cabinets are often made of polished rosewood or some other fancy wood, and may be finished with marqueterie. The interior of these is sometimes finished in white picked out with gold. Some of these cabinets are made to hang, others stand either on four open legs, or the lower part contains cupboards and drawers. Similar cabinets are constructed to hold music.

CHAPTER VII

TABLES

Dining-room Tables.—Plate LXXXV is a design for an extensible dining-room table. The plate shows details of construction and the method of fixing the screw which extends the framework, so that extra leaves can be fitted in. The principles of construction are the same in all non-folding tables. The upper part of the four (or more) legs is of rectangular form, and rails are fastened to these with mortise-and-tenon joints to form the side frame. This frame is strengthened, if necessary, by adding extra cross-pieces at intervals between the legs. The height of a dining-table is usually 2 feet 6 inches, and the width from 3 feet 6 inches to 4 feet.   There are many ways of fixing the top, the simplest is to fasten it by screws passed upwards through the frame.   The extension-screw is dispensed with in some tables, the frame-work being pulled out or pushed in by hand when leaves are inserted or removed.   The leaves are about 1½ foot wide, and are fitted together with dowels; mouldings are planted on their exposed edges to match that of the rest of the table.   Care must be taken, in constructing tables of long extension, to make the frame substantial, for when fully extended the strain in the centre is very great.   An extra leg is sometimes provided for insertion under the middle of the table to bear the extra strain.   The upper part of a dining-table leg is usually square, and the lower part may be square, octagonal, or circular, and moulded and carved in a variety of ways.

Fig. 1063.—Round Table

Fig. 1063 shows a small round table, the top being turned up so that the details of construction can be seen.   The top is built on a rectangular framework, and a moulded rim about 2 inches deep is planted round the edge.   It rests on a turned and carved shaft, which is supported by three claw-shaped feet.   A frame about 1 foot square is attached to the upper end of the shaft, and this fits into a frame of the same size in the under side of the top, the latter being pivoted on two thumb-screws.   By pulling a handle which moves two bolts, the top may be tilted into a vertical position to aid removal; it is taken off altogether by loosening the thumb-screws. When fitted into its place, the bolts catch in the frame after the manner of door bolts.   The table-top is made of 1-inch boards dowelled together, and is strengthened by a framework underneath, as shown in the illustration.   Round tables of this kind are not usually more than 5 or 6 feet in diameter.

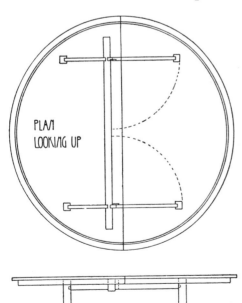

Fig. 1064.—Round Table with Folding Legs

Larger tables are made with four legs, and are so constructed that half the top takes off and two of the legs fold in.   The movable part fits in its place with dowels, and is secured by thumb-screws from underneath.   When the table is folded, it may be placed against the wall and used as a temporary sideboard.   The details of construction of such a table are shown in fig. 1064.   Oval tables are constructed in the same manner as round, but many, and especially those of Chippendale make, have four legs and do not fold.   Some round tables are made to take an extra leaf; when this is inserted they have an oval shape.

Massive tables of carved oak are generally placed in halls.   They are similar in design to dining-room tables, but the lower ends of the legs are sometimes connected with carved rails or composite turned work.

Drawing-room Tables.—The chief point to be noticed in the construction of tables and other furniture required for drawing-rooms is that they should be as light and elegant as possible. Buhl tables are perhaps the handsomest obtainable for drawing-rooms. The edges and certain parts of the legs are ornamented with brasswork, and the sides, tops, and legs are embellished with buhl or inlaid work. The edge of the top is usually curved, and the four sides are cut to match. The legs are also elegantly curved and tapered. The tops of some of these tables are movable, made of two flaps which fold over one another, and, when opened, can be turned round to form a card-table. Some of these tables have three or six legs. A very good effect is obtained by overlaying the top and sides of a table with inlayed fretwork, and pokerwork is sometimes used for commoner tables.

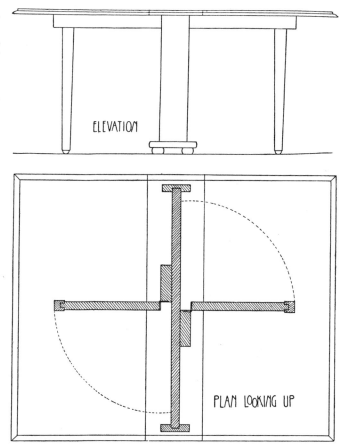

Fig. 1065.—The Sutherland Folding Table

The Sutherland folding table is shown in fig. 1065. The middle part of the table, which is about 6 inches wide, is supported at each end by a leg of the same width, formed out of a single board (plain or cut to pattern) or constructed of a number of pieces framed together. A folding flap is hinged to each side of this central part, and is supported by a leg, the upper end of which is fixed to a piece of wood about 18 inches long, 3 inches deep, and $1\frac{1}{2}$ inch thick. These are hinged to a board fixed under the centre-piece, and fold in on either side when the flaps are to be let down. A thumb moulding is cut round the edge of the top, and the abutting edges of the flaps and centre-piece are either left square or are jointed in one of the ways shown in fig. 1044.

Fig. 1066 shows a folding card-table, which may be made of rosewood and inlaid, or finished with buhl-work. The top is exactly square, and the four flaps,

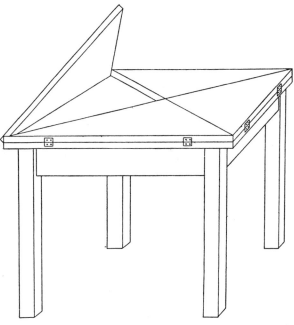

Fig. 1066.—Folding Card-table

which are hinged to it and fold over, should meet exactly in the centre. The top of the table and the inside of the flaps are covered with dark-green cloth, and a drawer is fitted underneath. The illustration shows the table in the rough; in practice the legs are curved or spindle-shaped, and the top and sides highly finished with ornamental work. Some tables are made with the top in the shape of a shamrock leaf, the three foils being flaps which can be let down. Such flaps are supported by small hinged brackets, or by pieces of wood which pull in and out from the centre. Other tables have hexagonal or octagonal tops and a corresponding number of legs.

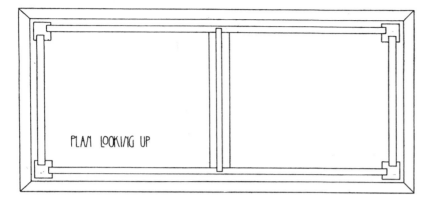

Library Tables.—Libraries and smoking-rooms are furnished with tables somewhat similar to those used in the dining-room, and also with tables for writing. The latter are provided with one or more drawers, and an oblong piece of stamped leather is let into the top. Fig. 1067 shows a plain writing-table, with two drawers; it is 4 feet long, 2 feet wide, and $2\frac{1}{4}$ feet high. The top is $1\frac{1}{2}$ inch thick, its edge is moulded, and stamped

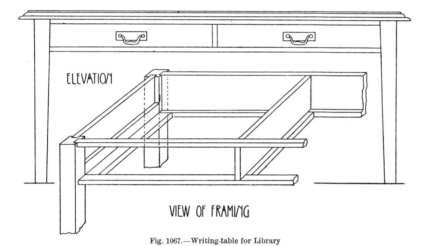

Fig. 1067.—Writing-table for Library

leather is let into it, leaving a margin 3 inches wide all round. The view of the left-hand end of the framework shows the method of fixing the drawers. This framework, with the exception of the legs, is made of 1-inch material; the latter are turned from $2\frac{1}{2}$-inch

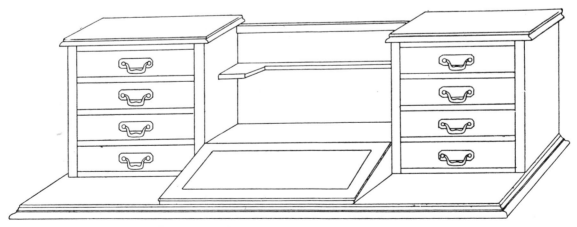

Fig. 1068.—Top of Writing-table with Nests of Drawers and Sloping Desk

scantling, and are left square at top, but the outside corners of the square parts are sometimes slightly rounded. The fronts of the drawers are 1 inch, and the backs and sides $\frac{1}{2}$ inch thick. The four sides of the drawer form its framework, and are dovetailed together.   A groove is ploughed on these sides about $\frac{1}{2}$ inch from the lower edge and receives the bottom.   The latter may also be grooved into a rectangular frame of 2-inch rails fixed to the interior of the drawer-frame.   The bars of wood upon which the drawers rest are called the runners.   Small blocks of wood about $1\frac{1}{2}$ inch square and $\frac{1}{2}$ inch thick are glued on to these, one near each end to act as guides and make the drawers slide in easily.   As the bottom is made as light as possible, it consists, in the case of large drawers, of two or more $\frac{3}{8}$-inch or $\frac{1}{4}$-inch panels grooved into a framework of thicker material.

Some writing-tables are fitted with a sloping top about 2 feet wide to form a desk. The back of this is about 6 inches, and the front 2 inches, above the top of the table; the top

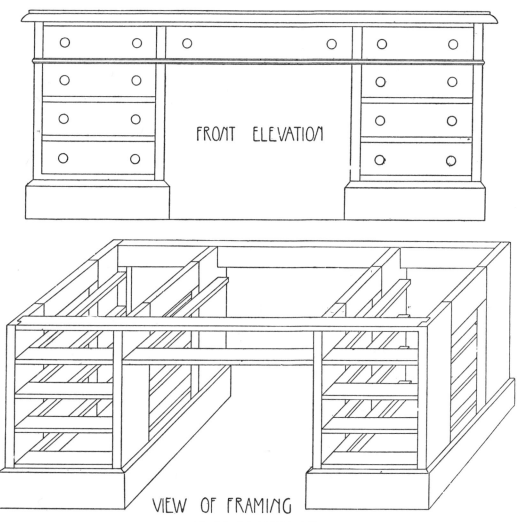

Fig. 1069.—Pedestal Writing-table

is hinged and fitted with a lock so that it can be used as a receptacle for letters, &c. Another form of writing-table is provided with two tiers of drawers, one on either side of the sloping desk (fig. 1068).

Fig. 1069 shows a more convenient kind of table, where the legs are replaced by two pedestals fitted with drawers. The details of the framework are shown in the view. The top together with the three uppermost drawers is sometimes made in one piece, and lifts completely off the two pedestals. It is fitted to the pedestals by four or more projecting knobs of wood 1 inch thick, which project from the latter and fit tightly into its under side. The drawers may be either locked separately, or a hinged flap locks across one edge, and a false flap is fastened to the other side for the sake of symmetry. The tops of some of these writing-tables and desks are fitted with roll-tops, which are made of laths about 1 inch wide, $\frac{1}{2}$ inch thick, and of semicircular section hinged together, or glued to strong canvas. The ends of these slide in curved grooves cut in the end-pieces which meet the back. The latter is about 18 inches high, and contains drawers, pigeon-holes, &c. In many desks the drawers in the pedestals are locked by closing the roll-top.

The tiers of drawers which form the pedestals of writing-tables are sometimes made separately, and used for storing butterflies, eggs, chemicals, and other scientific specimens. They are closed by a glazed door which locks across the front of the framework.

Fig. 1070.—Tables, &c., for Council Chamber

Fig. 1070 shows the tables and other furniture of a council chamber, designed by the editor. The rectangular table is placed on a raised dais, and is used by the chairman, vice-chairman, and clerk. The semicircular table in front of this is for the use of the surveyor and other officials, and the members of the council are seated around the semi-annular table. A drawer is provided for each councillor and official. All the tables and chairs are of oak, the chairs being upholstered in red morocco.

Altars or Communion Tables.—These are generally made of oak, and have the front and two sides carved and otherwise ornamented, and the back left plain. Plate LXXXVI shows an oak communion-table for a chapel, carried out from the editor's design.

CHAPTER VIII

CHAIRS, SOFAS, SETTLES, AND SEATS

Chairs.—Although chairs have an infinite variety of form, they are all constructed upon nearly the same principles. No. 1, fig. 1071, is an illustration of the framework of a chair suitable for a sitting-room. The hind part consists of two long pieces of squared stuff, to which are mortised two horizontal upper rails forming the back, a third at the level of the seat, and a fourth below. These back legs are usually curved backward above and below the seat, so that the chair-back has a slight slope and so that the feet are spread

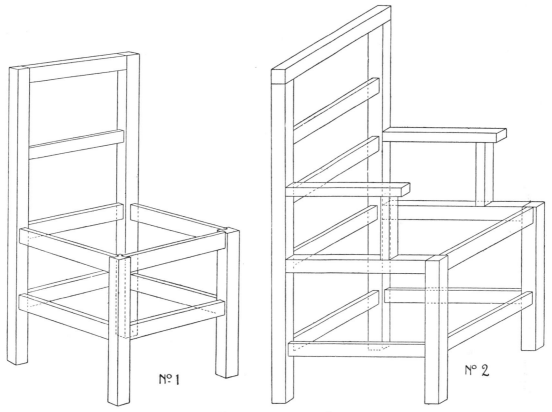

Fig. 1071.—Framework of Chairs

out sufficiently to prevent tilting. The front legs are joined by two rails, and are also fastened to the back by the same number. The tenons of the upper rails may come up flush with the top of the leg, as shown in the illustration, or can be fitted into an ordinary mortise. The width of the rails at the level of the seat depends upon the nature of the upholstery; if springs are to be fitted, they are about 3 inches wide. The bottom rails are omitted in some chairs of heavy build, or the side pairs of legs are connected by rails and the middle of these joined by a cross-piece.

All the parts of bedroom chairs, with the exception of the backs, are, as a rule, turned. The two back legs project above the seat to form the back, and are joined by two horizontal bars, which are slightly curved and joined to the vertical pieces by shallow mortises cut in the latter. The joint is further strengthened by screws passed from the front through counter-sunk holes, the heads being afterwards covered by small turned beads glued in, or, if the chair is to be painted, the holes can be filled with wooden plugs. The lower rails are turned, and their rounded ends fit into corresponding holes bored in the legs, where they are secured by glue. Sometimes only the front legs are turned, the back legs being left square and bent slightly outwards. The seats of such chairs are made of four flat pieces of wood about 1 inch thick mortised together, the front and back pieces overlapping the other two, and the back piece being shorter than that at the front. The corners and edges are slightly rounded, and sometimes the front piece is curved, as are also the sides. The front legs fit into holes bored in the under side of the seat, and the back legs are fitted to the seat by grooves $\frac{1}{2}$ inch deep cut in the former. Rounded backs are made by cutting the upper ends of the back legs to form part of a circle, and fitting across these a curved piece of wood. This is attached by mortise-and-tenon joints, or by dowels. The lower cross-bar is cut in a similar manner, so that, when the four are joined together, the back has the form of a segment of a circle or ellipse.

Drawing-room chairs are framed in a somewhat similar manner. Turned or fretted bars are sometimes inserted in the back, either horizontally or vertically, or part of the back is upholstered. The legs are squared, tapered, and slightly curved; or they are also turned and fluted, or left plain and carved.

No. 2, fig. 1071, shows the framework of an arm-chair. The only difference between this and No. 1 is that the back is higher, the seat larger, and four extra rails forming the arms are added. The latter may be upholstered, or not, according to the design of the chair; turned spindles are sometimes inserted between them and the seat. The back of the arm-chair is sometimes slightly curved, and the seat may be made of a large piece of stamped leather nailed across, without springs or other upholstery.

Dining-room chairs are now largely made of plain oak, the legs being square and tapering, the side and back rails flat, and the latter slightly curved. The wood may be darkened with ammonia, or stained dark-green, and the seat upholstered in leather. The backs of chairs of this type are not upholstered, but are generally made with top and bottom rails, the intermediate space being filled in with flat bars about 1 inch wide.

In office chairs and others of a similar type the four legs are mortised to the wooden seat, which is made slightly hollow towards the middle part. The curved back is made up of several pieces, which are cut to form a curve and mortised or dowelled together. It is attached to the seat by a series of turned or square vertical bars fixed by mortises, the two at the ends in front being stouter than the others. An extra piece of curved wood with a rounded edge is sometimes fixed to the middle part of the top of the back to serve as a shoulder-rest. When the seat is made to swivel round, the legs bend inwards, and meet at a small block of wood faced with metal, upon which the seat revolves. Office chairs are sometimes slightly upholstered instead of being left altogether plain.

The framework of an easy-chair is almost the same as that of an arm-chair, but the side rails which support the seat are much wider, the legs are shorter and thicker, and the seat stretches farther back. The back is not so high, and is made to slope slightly. The space between the arms and seat may be left open, filled with carved or turned work, or covered with upholstery. Some settees are made after the manner of large easy-chairs, wide enough to contain two or three persons; the framework of such is the same, but the seat and back are strengthened by additional cross-pieces.

Music Stools.—These are made either with a fixed top, or with a top that can be raised. The former have four legs and the top is round or square. The legs sometimes slope slightly outwards towards the feet to obtain greater stability. In the plainer kind of stool, the seat is made of $1\frac{1}{2}$-inch boards with moulded edges, and of round, square, or oblong shape. If round, it is turned on the lathe out of one piece. If it is to be upholstered, a $\frac{1}{2}$-inch rebate is cut all round, and the upholstery is fastened to it with brass-headed nails and finished off with gimp. The legs are either square or turned, and are screwed into the under side of the seat; they are strengthened near the lower ends by turned cross-rails. The coarse screws cut at the top of the legs are not turned on the lathe when they are being shaped, but are made subsequently with the aid of a "box-screw". This is a

PLATE LXXXV

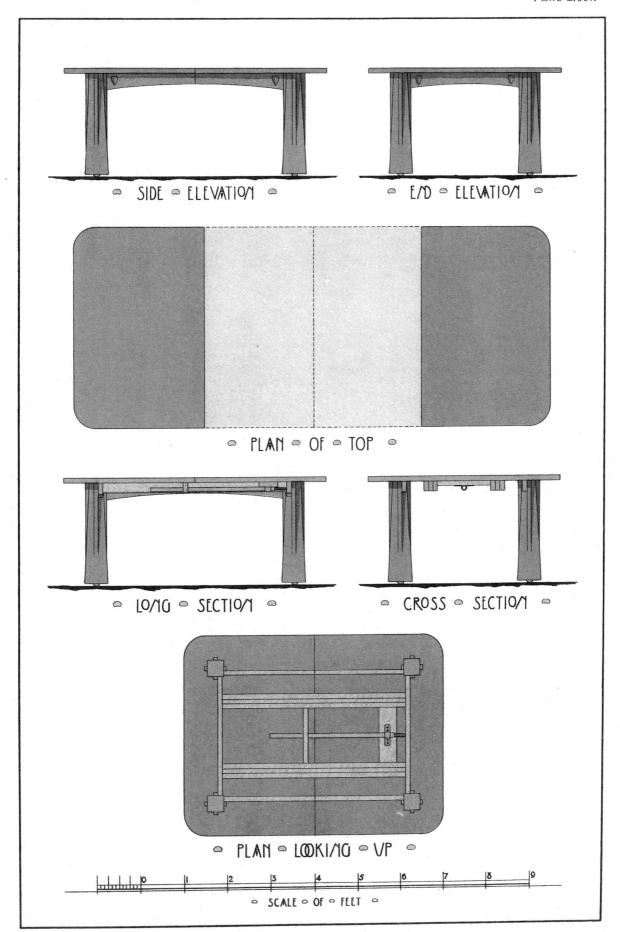

SIDE ○ ELEVATION

E/D ○ ELEVATION

PLAN ○ OF ○ TOP

LO/G ○ SECTION

CROSS ○ SECTION

PLAN ○ LOOKING ○ VP

SCALE ○ OF ○ FEET

DESIGN FOR DINING TABLE

PLATE LXXXVI

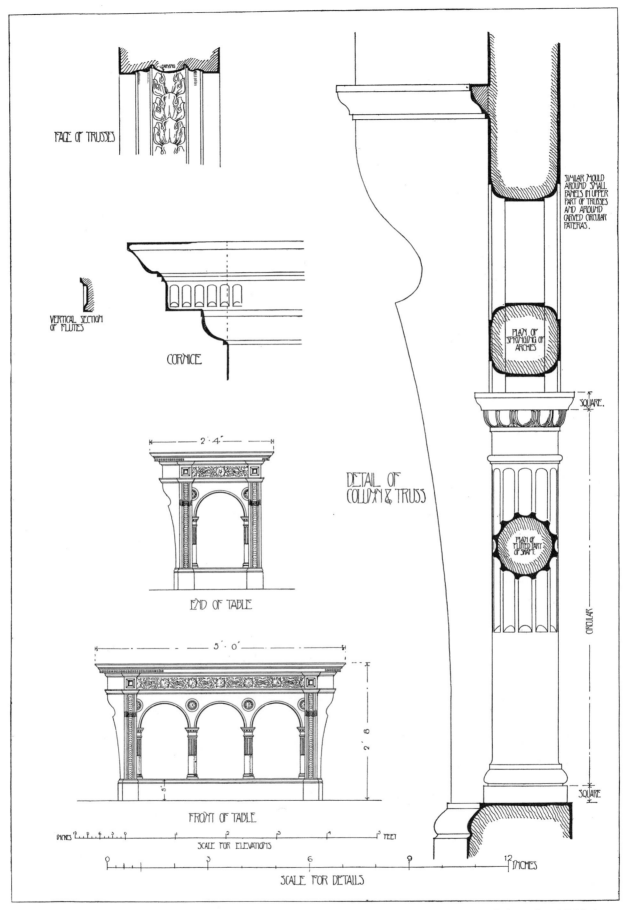

FACE OF TRUSSES

VERTICAL SECTION OF FLUTES

CORNICE

SIMILAR MOULD AROUND SMALL PANELS IN UPPER PART OF TRUSSES AND AROUND CARVED CIRCULAR PATERAS.

PLAN OF SPRINGING OF ARCHES

2·4″

END OF TABLE

DETAIL OF COLUMN & TRUSS

PLAN OF FLUTED PART OF SHAFT.

SQUARE.

CIRCULAR

SQUARE.

5·0″

2·8″

5″

FRONT OF TABLE

INCHES   FEET
SCALE FOR ELEVATIONS

0   6   9   12 INCHES
SCALE FOR DETAILS

G. L. Sutcliffe, A.R.I.B.A.

OAK COMMUNION TABLE FOR CHAPEL

rectangular block of wood with a handle at either end, and pierced by a hole in which a female screw corresponding to the male screw is cut. The top end of the leg is turned down for about 1½ or 2 inches till it fits into one end of the hole, when it is pushed in and turned round at the same time, the screw being cut by a small knife inside. This method of joining legs is only used for light pieces of furniture and fancy tables, the legs being usually attached by mortise-and-tenon joints.

Stools with movable seats have a stout turned pillar to which three curved feet are fastened by mortise-and-tenon joints, meeting it about 6 inches from the ground. The top of the pillar is cut off flat and a hole 9 inches deep bored down it. A steel female screw is fixed into this, and a corresponding male screw about 9 inches long is fastened to the under side of the top. The latter is always circular and upholstered.

Sofas and Settees.— The framework of a sofa is shown in No. 1, fig. 1072. The four legs, which are represented simply as square blocks of wood, are fitted to the front and back rails with mortise-and-tenon joints. The upper part where the mortises are cut is generally made pretty stout to ensure strength, and any resulting clumsiness is concealed by the upholstery. The lower part is tapered, carved, or turned. The front and back rails are strengthened by an additional cross-piece placed midway, and a similar cross-piece is fitted to the back, which is other-

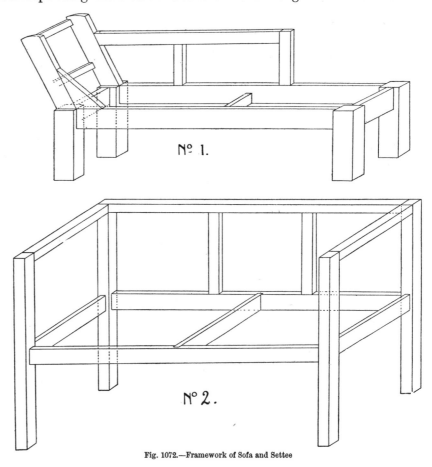

Fig. 1072.—Framework of Sofa and Settee

wise similar to the arm of an easy-chair. A method of fastening the head of the sofa is shown in the illustration; it consists of two rails mortised to the front and back legs in a slanting position, and strengthened by two cross-pieces. These rails are generally carved, and the front edges of both moulded. The outside of the front rail may also be carved. The top rail of the back is sometimes curved downwards until it meets the back rail of the lower frame, being made of two or more pieces mortised or dowelled together. The space between the two is sometimes filled with turned bars. In order to obtain lightness, each pair of legs is sometimes joined by two slight rails placed 2 or 3 inches apart instead of by a solid rail.

The framework of the simple square settee is shown in No. 2, fig. 1072. As all the woodwork of this is usually hidden by upholstery which reaches nearly down to the floor, it is made of common wood and receives no high degree of finish. The four legs are turned at the lower end and left square at the upper. The four rails which form the seat are mortised into the sides of the legs, as are also the three upper rails which form the back and ends. The back can be further strengthened, if necessary, by inserting two diagonal bars. These settees are made in a great variety of forms, from that above described to the lighter and more elegant pieces of furniture which are embellished with turned work and only partly upholstered. Sometimes the four legs which form the end-pieces are turned and the seat-frame inserted in notches cut in these, and so upholstered that the lower part of the latter and all the legs are visible.

Settees for billiard-rooms are framed similarly to arm-chairs (see No. 2, fig. 1071). They are generally made about 6 or 7 feet long, and either straight or bent to suit corners. The woodwork of a billiard-room settee is shown in fig. 1073. The parts are more massive than those of ordinary settees. The legs are made of 3-inch scantling, those at the front being turned, whilst the other pair are bent slightly backwards. The settee stands on a platform about 8 inches high, and of such a size that there is a margin 1 foot wide at the front and sides. The two front corners of the platform are slightly rounded. When the settee is not intended to be placed on a platform, the legs are made longer and a foot-rest is fastened to the front about 6 inches from the floor. This is made of 1-inch stuff with rounded edges; it is fastened at the back into grooves cut in the front legs, and in front is supported on stout turned feet.

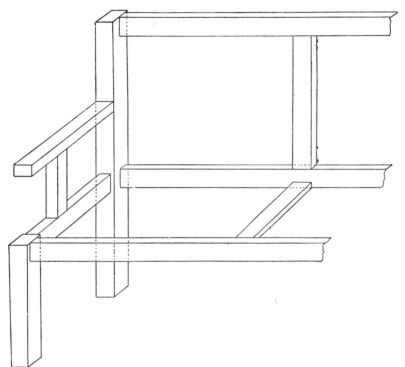

Fig. 1073.—Framework of Billiard-room Settee

Seats for railway-stations, waiting-rooms, public offices, &c., are made in the same manner as billiard-room settees, and sometimes have an additional arm in the middle.

Settles. — No. 1, fig. 1074, is an illustration of a seat or settle in darkened oak, suitable for a hall. The sides are made of 1½- or 2-inch stuff, and grooves are cut in them to receive the seat, which is of the same thickness. The seat is ½ inch less in width than the sides, and comes up flush at the front, thus leaving a space ½ inch wide for the back. It may be attached to the sides by cutting at each end a rounded tenon 2 inches wide. These tenons project about 1½ inch through mortises cut in the end-pieces. Half-round holes are cut through these projecting pieces so that they are flush with the sides. When the seat is in its place, a peg made by cutting a piece of tapering turned wood in a longitudinal direction is hammered in tight. This is shown in the illustration, and holds the sides and seat firmly together. To form the back, two horizontal rails are dovetailed to the sides, one at the bottom and the other at the top. The inner edges of these are grooved to fit a series of vertical boards, which are ½ inch thick and chamfered at the edges. The top edge of the settle is moulded or left square.

Some settles are made five or six feet high. The back of these is upholstered for about 3 feet above the seat, and the remainder of the space above is filled with solid or fretted panels. A narrow shelf for china, &c., is sometimes fixed near the top.

Settles (No. 2, fig. 1074) are sometimes made of only two end-pieces and a seat. The former are made of 1½-inch oak, cut to any suitable shape.   Settles of this kind serve as seats or for holding large pieces of china.

Another kind of settle which is very suitable for halls, has a seat 4 or 5 feet wide, and arms at the ends.   The lower part forms a box, and is 1 foot deep, the lid being the seat.   The sides and back are similar to those of an arm-chair.   The four legs are usually of 2-inch scantling; the two back legs project above the seat and are joined by two horizontal 1-inch rails, one at the top and the other nearly at the level of the seat. Two rails, which are fitted with panels, join each pair of legs and form the sides of the box.   Panels of ½-inch stuff are grooved to these.   The framing of the lid is formed of 1-inch stuff, and is 2 or 3 inches wide. This kind of settle may be left plain, or finished with flat or chip carving.

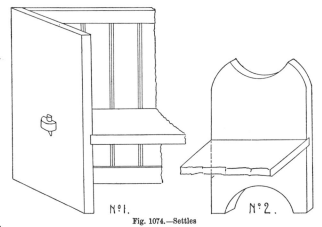

Fig. 1074.—Settles

Settles which are intended for drawing-rooms are similar in structural details to those made for the hall, but they are much lighter, and the greater part of the back and sides is upholstered. Many are fitted with a narrow shelf at the top, and the back is curved instead of being square.

Seats. — Under this heading come seats which are fastened in corners, alcoves, and windows, and are part of the fixtures of the house.   The simplest seat of this kind is made by fixing a board 14 inches wide and 1½ inch thick across the alcove or corner at a distance of about 18 inches from the floor, and supported on shaped brackets or legs.   The edge of this board may be rounded or moulded.   If the seat is longer than 3 feet, it is supported by a rail under the front edge, or by a leg in the middle of the length.   The top of the seat is covered with a cushion, and the space beneath may be concealed by a hanging of cloth or other material, or filled up with a skirting-board or panelling to match that of the rest of the room.   Seats in the recesses of windows usually have the backs and elbows panelled or filled with match-boarding between the top of the seat and the window-sill, and the seat itself sometimes forms the lid of a locker.   A seat of this kind is shown in the drawing-room bay of the house illustrated in Plates XIX and XXIV.   When a seat is fitted into a polygonal bay window, it is made in sections, which are mitred at each corner.   It is supported at the ends and each corner by legs, and is further strengthened at the corners by a transverse rail mortised into the leg.   If the space below the seat is shut in by wood-work, legs will not be required.

CHAPTER IX

MISCELLANEOUS FURNITURE

Chests of Drawers.—The frame of a chest of drawers is shown in fig. 1075.   The rails are all made of 1-inch stuff, but in some frames the runners and rails which separate the drawers are made of ¾-inch or ½-inch boards.   The front of the frame is fitted together first, the horizontal rails being attached to the end-pieces by grooves ½ inch deep, but coming up flush in front.   The top rail is usually dovetailed into the end uprights.   The runners upon which the drawers slide are mortised into the horizontal rails in front, and grooved to the uprights at the back. The uprights extend about 6 inches below the lowest runners, so that a plinth of that width which raises the frame above the ground can be attached to them by screws passed through from the inside. The inside edges of the two outside uprights of the back, and both edges of the middle upright, are grooved to receive the back, which is made of $\frac{3}{8}$-inch stuff planed down at the edges to fit the grooves. The two side uprights lap over the edges of the two back uprights, and are attached to them by screws. When the frame has been put together, the sides are filled in and the back inserted. The boards which form the sides are fastened by screws passed through the runners. The back

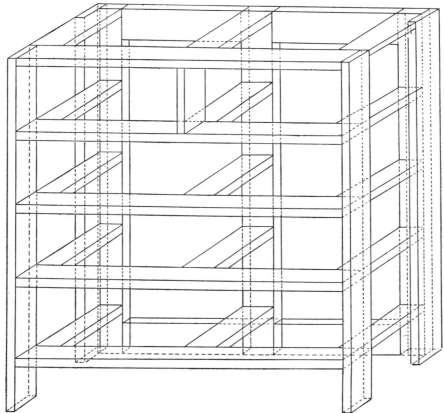

Fig. 1075.—Framework of Chest of Drawers

consists either of ordinary panels let into the grooves, or of pieces of match-boarding. An extra horizontal rail is sometimes inserted half-way up to give additional strength.

The top is of 1-inch boards dowelled together, and the edges of its front and sides are moulded, the back edge being left square. It is attached to the upper horizontal rails by screws passed upwards from underneath. A slightly different method of making the sides is sometimes employed. The end runners are cut so that they come up flush with the four vertical rails. The sides are then made separately and fastened over these rails by screws passed through from the inside, their front edges coming up flush with the edges of the vertical rails. This latter method, however, involves waste of material.

In making the drawers, the fronts are first cut out of 1-inch stuff and accurately fitted to their places in the frame. The usual method of constructing a drawer suitable for a chest of drawers, table, wardrobe, or cabinet is shown in fig. 1076. The sides are cut out of $\frac{1}{2}$-inch and the back out of $\frac{3}{8}$-inch stuff. The front overlaps the two sides and is joined to them by dovetails. The sides overlap the end and are also attached by dovetails. The method of fixing the bottom of the drawer is shown in No. 2. A groove somewhat narrower than the bottom-board is cut on the inside of the two sides near the lower edge. The bottom-board is then cut out about $\frac{1}{2}$ inch wider than the inside of the drawer, and its sides planed down to fit the grooves. Another method is to fasten a strip of wood $\frac{1}{2}$ inch wide on both sides close to the lower edge, and another narrower strip $\frac{1}{4}$ inch above this, thus forming a groove $\frac{1}{4}$ inch wide into which the bottom slides. The projecting corner of the upper strip is rounded for the sake of convenience, as it will be inside the drawer. In the case of very long drawers, the bottom is strengthened by a rail of wood 4 inches wide and $\frac{3}{8}$ inch thick, fastened from front to back. Thin blocks of wood about 2 inches square are glued to the upper side of each of the horizontal front bars of the frame to prevent the drawers being pushed in too far, and similar blocks are sometimes glued to the runners to make the drawers slide in easily.

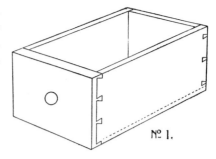

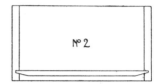

Fig. 1076.—Details of Drawer

Wash-stands are made similarly to the writing-table already described, and the drawers are fitted in the same manner. The frame is usually made to receive a top of marble or tiles, with sides and back of similar material about 8 inches high. Two vertical pieces are screwed to the back of the frame, and three horizontal rails are mortised to these, the inside edges being rebated. These three rails are fixed at such a distance apart that the tiles just fit them, and they are all beaded or moulded at the edges. The outer edge of the upper rails is generally cut to some pattern. A cupboard closed by two doors is sometimes made instead of drawers. This would be constructed by fixing a bottom-board, two end-pieces, and a back to the legs and fitting a partition at the centre; the bottom-board may be about 8 inches from the floor.

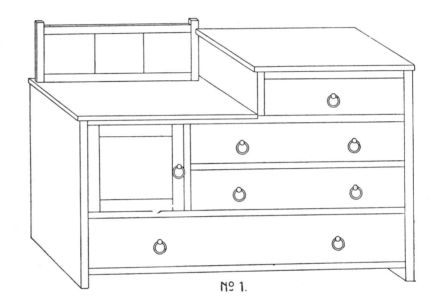

Nº 1.

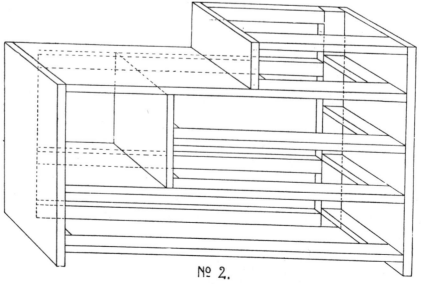

Nº 2.

Fig. 1077.—Combined Dressing-table and Wash-stand

Dressing-tables are also constructed similarly to writing-tables, but two supports for a mirror and a few extra drawers are sometimes added to the top. No. 1, fig. 1077, is a combined wash-stand, chest of drawers, and dressing-table, and No. 2 a view of the frame. The top of the left-hand portion is made of marble, and a light frame is attached to the back and fitted with tiles. The top of the right-hand part is used as a dressing-table, and a mirror is hinged to two uprights, which are mortised to it, one near each end. The runners for the drawers are fixed as already described. The door of the cupboard is made of two stiles and two rails, to which a panel is attached by grooves. The tops of chests of drawers are sometimes fitted as dressing-tables, a few small drawers, some shelves, and a swing mirror being added.

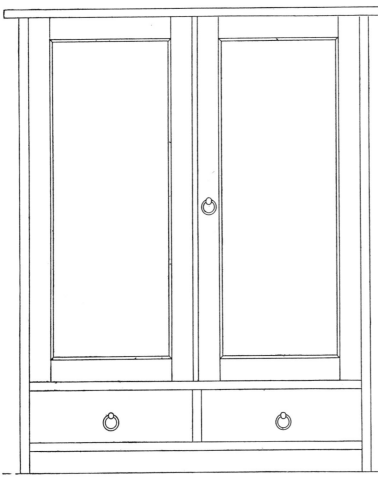

Fig. 1078.—Elevation of Small Wardrobe

Wardrobes.—Fig. 1078 is the front elevation of the simplest kind of wardrobe, containing two doors (which close two compartments) and two drawers below. The framework of this wardrobe is shown in fig. 1079. The two shelves between which the drawers are fixed are attached to the sides by grooves cut in the latter, but are $\frac{3}{4}$ inch narrower than the sides, so that a space is left to receive the back. The shelves in the left-hand portion are set back 1 inch at the front to allow the door to fit in, and they are also recessed $\frac{3}{4}$ inch behind to receive the back. The door-frames are made of 1-inch stiles and rails, which are grooved to receive the panels; the stiles and rails are either moulded on the solid or a small moulding is planted around after the doors have been framed together. The panels are sometimes fixed without grooves, a narrow strip of wood being fixed at the back and a moulding in front with the panel between the two. The back is made of vertical stiles $\frac{3}{4}$ inch thick and 3 or 4 inches wide, fixed about 1½ feet apart, and panelled with thinner boards. Instead of being fixed, the shelves are sometimes, for the sake of convenience, made to slide in and out on small runners. In this case, each shelf is fitted with a back and sides 4 or 5 inches high to prevent the articles falling out, and the doors are hung over the side frame, as shown in No. 2, fig. 1045. A rail 3 inches wide is fixed inside the right-hand part near the top (see fig. 1079), and hooks are screwed to this for hanging clothes, &c. Wardrobes of simple design are often made of ash, stained and varnished, or of some soft wood stained or painted, but oak, walnut, maple, mahogany, &c., are also used.

Larger wardrobes contain three or four divisions, some of which are left open for hanging clothes, &c., whilst others are fitted with shelves or drawers. The doors are

PLATE LXXXVII

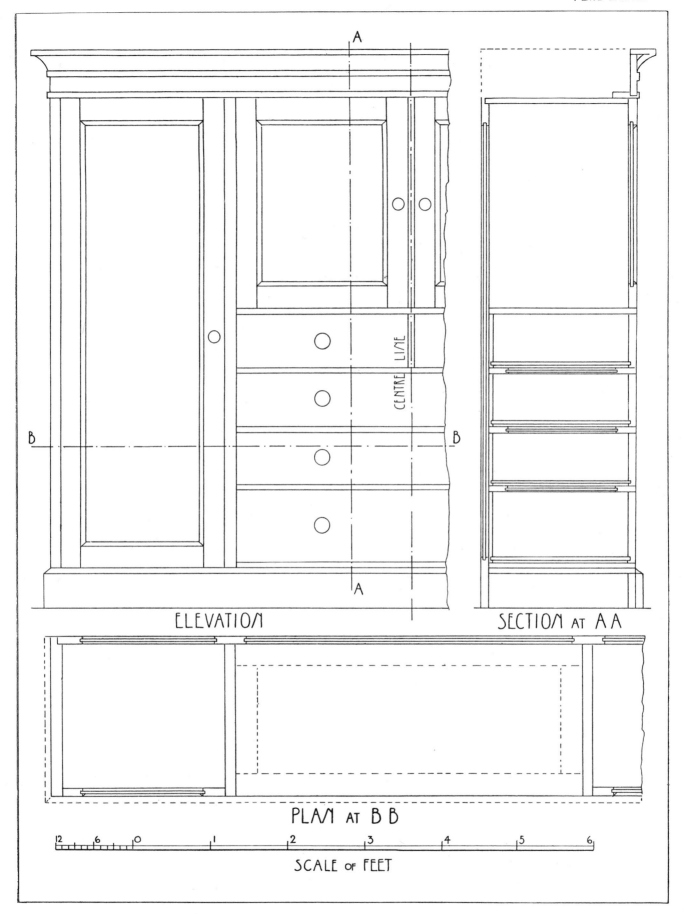

ELEVATION

SECTION AT A A

PLAN AT B B

SCALE OF FEET

DESIGN FOR WARDROBE WITH DRAWERS

also fitted with mirrors, and a moulded or carved cornice is added. This kind of wardrobe is generally made in several pieces for convenience in removal. The top lifts off, and the body is composed of two or three pieces, which are fitted to the base. The joint is fitted in the same manner as that of the top of the pedestal writing-table described in Chapter VII. Small blocks of wood about 2 inches square are glued on the under side of each vertical piece, one near each corner. These fit into hollow spaces at the corners of the base. The latter is made of four pieces of 1-inch material of the right width, fastened together and strengthened by a cross-piece in the middle. Similar pieces are fixed flat on the top of this, and the blocks should fit into the corners made by these and a cross-piece fixed in the proper position. This and other similar framework can be strengthened by gluing small blocks of wood 3 inches long and $\frac{1}{2}$ or $\frac{3}{4}$ inch square

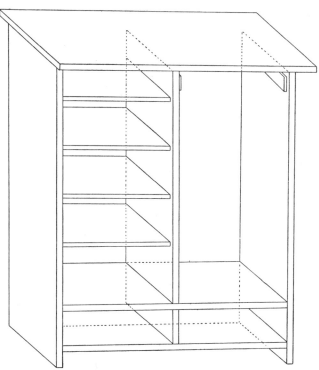

Fig. 1079.—View of Framing of Small Wardrobe

at short distances apart along the angle-joint. When the vertical pieces are placed in position on the base, they are fastened together by screws passed through the sides. The top is an open frame, with square or slightly rounded front corners, and made of moulding. It also has a transverse rail across the middle to add strength. It is attached to the vertical pieces by blocks of wood in the same manner as the base.

Plate LXXXVII shows the front elevation, section, and plan of a large wardrobe with two long cupboards, a tier of drawers, and two shorter cupboards enclosing shelves. It is constructed in one piece, but the top and bottom can be made movable, as already described. The framework consists of two end-pieces and two middle-pieces, which form the sides of the longer cupboards, and should reach to the ground. The partitions between the drawers and the runners are the same as those in a chest of drawers. The partitions between the two shorter cupboards and two upper drawers extend to the back. There is one sliding tray with a back and sides in each of these two cupboards; it has a projecting ledge at the sides, and this fits into grooves cut in the partitions. Several grooves are cut in the latter, so that the height of the shelf can be varied.

The back is made of 1-inch framing, to which intermediate panels are grooved. The stiles of this framing are best if placed one at each end, and one to meet each of the three partition boards which divide the cupboards. Similar horizontal rails are fixed, one level with the top and the other to meet the base. The latter consists of a plinth with a moulded edge and mitred corners. The doors are panelled, fitted with moulding, and hinged so that they are flush with the partition boards. The top consists of thin boards screwed to the tops of the partitions, and the moulded cornice is screwed to this. When the moulding projects very much, a board is screwed to the top so that it slopes outwards, and the lengths of moulding, which may be two or three deep, are screwed to this.

Hat-stands.—The front and side elevations of a hat-stand suitable for a hall are shown in fig. 1080. The table and drawer are constructed as already described. There are projecting pieces of wood at the ends of the front and back at the level of the bottom of the drawer.   The ends of these are joined by circular rails about 1 inch diameter, and serve as umbrella and stick stands.   A shelf is fitted to the lower part of the table a few inches from the floor, and rectangular portions of this are made hollow near the ends, and fitted with shallow zinc or enamelled iron troughs to receive the ends of the sticks and umbrellas.   Sometimes portions are cut completely out of the shelf, and zinc troughs 2 or 3 inches deep fitted in.   The upper edge of the trough is provided with a $\frac{1}{2}$-inch flange to prevent it from falling through.   The back is composed of two vertical pieces, which are screwed to the back of the table.   These are joined by three horizontal rails, one at the top, one at the level of the table, and a third about 1 foot above.   Four ornamental tiles are fixed between the two latter, being fitted into rebates and fixed by narrow strips of wood.   The upper edge of the upper horizontal rail is cut into the pattern shown in No. 1, and flat pieces of wood are attached to its middle and ends.   The mirror in the centre is of bevelled plate, and is fixed in a frame made of four pieces of wood rebated behind and mitred at the corners.   The mirror-frame is held in position in the outer frame by four short pieces of wood mortised to it and to the latter.   The hat-pegs are either wooden pegs turned with knobs at the end, or of iron or brass.

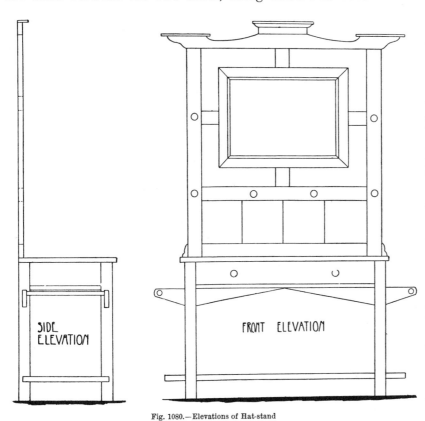

Fig. 1080.—Elevations of Hat-stand

A more compact variation of this kind of hat-stand may be constructed by doing without the table.   A wooden base about 5 inches high and 9 inches wide is made out of 2-inch stuff.   A zinc trough with a $\frac{1}{2}$-inch flange is fitted to the hollow part of the base, and two vertical pieces are mortised to the latter to form the frame of the back.   Two legs of the same height as those in fig. 1080 are mortised to the front part.   A rail is mortised between the upper ends of the front legs, which are also joined to the back rails in the same manner.   A fourth rail is added to the back, and a table-top with a drawer is fastened to the middle part of these four rails, leaving an open space at each end for the insertion of sticks and umbrellas.   The rest of the back may be built up as shown in fig. 1080.

Hat-stands are also made with a table occupying only half of the front, the rest being intended for umbrellas, or with no table at all, there being a curved projecting arm at each end to hold the umbrellas.

Mantel-pieces.—Wood mantel-pieces are now largely used, and an example, designed by the editor for the dining-room of a house at Hindhead (Surrey), is given in Plate LXXXVIII.   It is of oak, oil-polished.   The panelled framing is $\frac{7}{8}$ inch thick, and the shelf and cornice are built up as shown in the details.

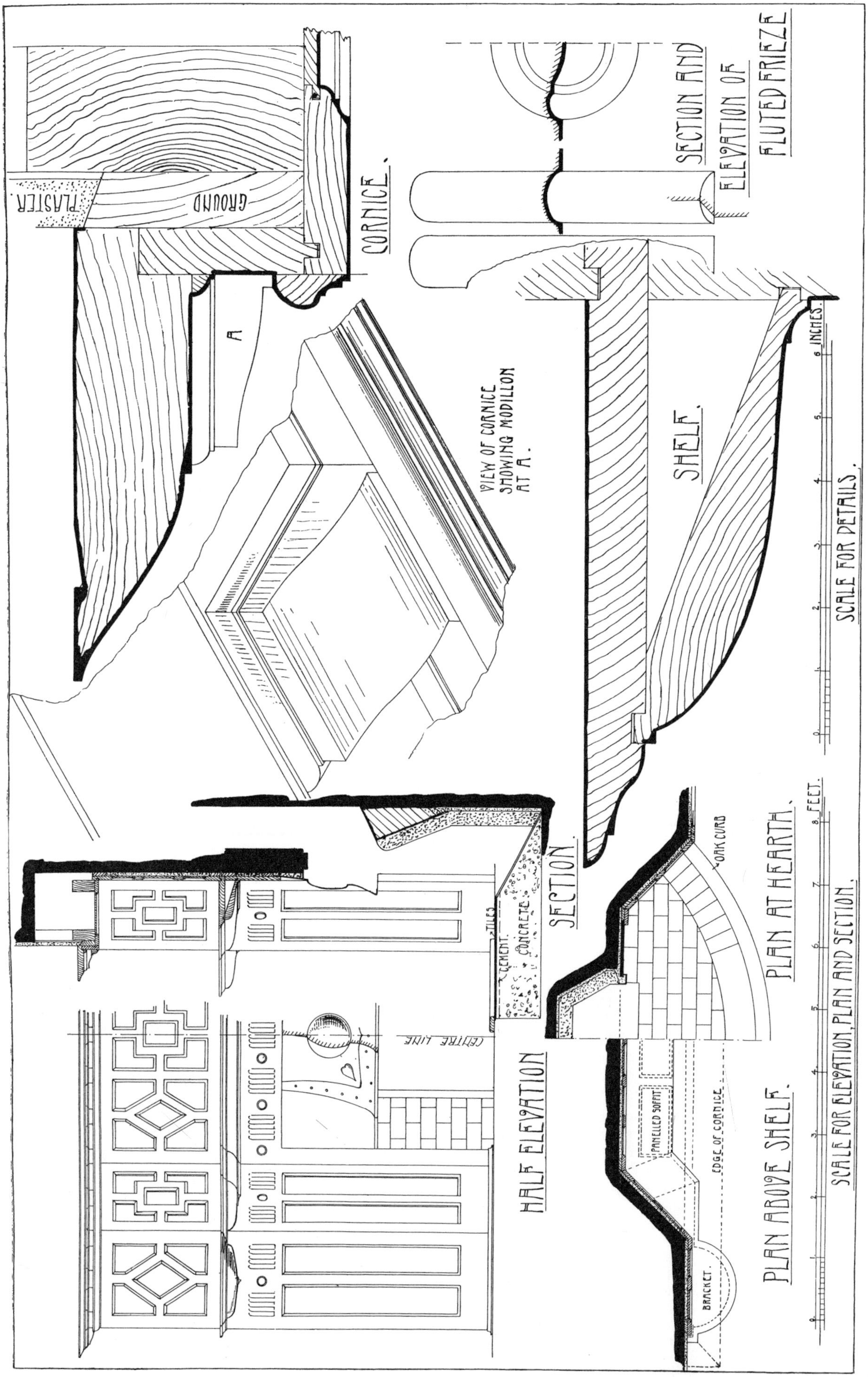

PLATE LXXXVIII

G. L. Sutcliffe, A.R.I.B.A.

CORNICE.

PLASTER

GROUND

SECTION AND
ELEVATION OF
FLUTED FRIEZE

A

VIEW OF CORNICE
SHOWING MODILLON
AT A.

SHELF.

6 INCHES

5

4

SCALE FOR DETAILS.

3

2

1

0

SECTION.

CEMENT.
CONCRETE.
TILES
CENTRE LINE

HALF ELEVATION

OAK CURB

PLAN AT HEARTH.

FEET.

8

7

6

5

SCALE FOR ELEVATION, PLAN AND SECTION.

PANELLED SOFFIT.

EDGE OF CORNICE.

PLAN ABOVE SHELF.

3

2

1

0

BRACKET.

OAK MANTELPIECE